SENSE AND SENSIBILITY

If you have strong feelings, is it better to express them, eagerly and passionately, to the whole world? Is it wise? And if you always show the world a calm face and a quiet voice, does this mean there is no passion, no fire in your heart?

When the Dashwood sisters have to move to Devon with their widowed mother, they are sad to leave the family home, now owned by their wealthy half-brother. The girls are quite poor, but they still have several admirers. There is shy Edward Ferrars, the romantic and handsome Mr Willoughby, the sad and silent Colonel Brandon.

But the course of true love does not run smoothly at first. Hopes of marriage disappear, guilty secrets come to light, hearts are broken. But which sister feels it more? Calm and sensible Elinor, smiling bravely and saying not a word – or romantic Marianne, sobbing wildly and passionately all night long…

D1106144

OXFORD BOOKWORMS LIBRARY

Classics

Sense and Sensibility

Stage 5 (1800 headwords)

Series Editor: Jennifer Bassett
Founder Editor: Tricia Hedge
Activities Editors: Jennifer Bassett and Christine Lindop

JANE AUSTEN

Sense and Sensibility

Retold by
Clare West

Illustrated by
Elena Selivonova

OXFORD UNIVERSITY PRESS

OXFORD
UNIVERSITY PRESS

Great Clarendon Street, Oxford, OX2 6DP, United Kingdom

Oxford University Press is a department of the University of Oxford.
It furthers the University's objective of excellence in research, scholarship,
and education by publishing worldwide. Oxford is a registered trade
mark of Oxford University Press in the UK and in certain other countries

This simplified edition © Oxford University Press 2016

The moral rights of the author have been asserted

First published in Oxford Bookworms 2002

10 9 8

No unauthorized photocopying

All rights reserved. No part of this publication may be reproduced,
stored in a retrieval system, or transmitted, in any form or by any means,
without the prior permission in writing of Oxford University Press, or as
expressly permitted by law, by licence or under terms agreed with the
appropriate reprographics rights organization. Enquiries concerning
reproduction outside the scope of the above should be sent to the ELT
Rights Department, Oxford University Press, at the address above

You must not circulate this work in any other form and you must
impose this same condition on any acquirer

Links to third party websites are provided by Oxford in good faith and
for information only. Oxford disclaims any responsibility for the materials
contained in any third party website referenced in this work

ISBN: 978 0 19 461442 9   Book
ISBN: 978 0 19 462119 9   Book and audio pack

Printed in China

Word count (main text): 24345

For more information on the Oxford Bookworms Library,
visit www.oup.com/elt/gradedreaders

ACKNOWLEDGEMENTS

Illustrations by: Elena Selivonova/Beehive Illustration

CONTENTS

PEOPLE IN THIS STORY

Mrs Dashwood a widow, living in Devonshire
Elinor Dashwood ⎫
Marianne Dashwood ⎬ Mrs Dashwood's daughters
Margaret Dashwood ⎭
Mr John Dashwood Mrs Dashwood's stepson
Mrs John Dashwood (Fanny) John Dashwood's wife, and
   sister-in-law to the Dashwood girls
Edward Ferrars Fanny Dashwood's brother
Robert Ferrars Edward's younger brother
Mrs Ferrars mother to Edward, Robert, and Fanny
Sir John Middleton the Dashwoods' neighbour in
   Devonshire
Lady Middleton Sir John's wife
Mrs Jennings Lady Middleton's mother
Mrs Charlotte Palmer Lady Middleton's sister
Mr Palmer Charlotte's husband
Miss Anne Steele ⎫
              ⎬ distant cousins of Mrs Jennings'
Miss Lucy Steele ⎭
Colonel Brandon Sir John Middleton's friend
John Willoughby a young man
Mrs Smith an elderly relation of Willoughby's

Chapter One

The Dashwood Family

For very many years there had been Dashwoods living in Sussex, in the south of England. The family owned a large area of land around their country house, Norland Park. Recently the head of the family, an unmarried man of great age, had invited into his home his nephew, who was expected to inherit the house and land, with his wife and children. The nephew, Mr Henry Dashwood, and his wife behaved kindly and thoughtfully towards the old gentleman, not from interest in his fortune, but from goodness of heart, so that he was able to spend his last years comfortably with these pleasant and cheerful companions.

By his first wife, Mr Henry Dashwood had one son, John; by his present wife, three daughters. John, a respectable, serious young man, had received a large inheritance from his mother, and had also added to his wealth by his own marriage. To him, therefore, the Norland fortune was not as important as to his sisters, who had very little money of their own.

When the old gentleman died, it was discovered that he had not left his fortune to Henry Dashwood to do what he liked with, but only to use during his lifetime. On Henry Dashwood's death, the inheritance would pass to his son John, and to John's son, a child of four years old. The old man had become fond of the small boy on his occasional visits to Norland, and so a spoilt child was preferred to Henry Dashwood's gentle wife and daughters, in spite of their years of loving care. No unkindness had been intended, however, and as a sign of his affection for the girls, the old gentleman left them one thousand pounds each.

At first Mr Henry Dashwood was bitterly disappointed, as he had wanted the fortune more for his wife and daughters than for himself. But he soon realized that if he was careful with money in the next few years, he could save enough to provide generously for his family. Unfortunately, he did not live to carry out this plan, as he survived his uncle by only one year, and ten thousand pounds was all that remained for his widow and daughters.

Just before his death, he sent for his son, and begged him to take care of his stepmother and sisters. Mr John Dashwood had not the strong feelings of the rest of the family, but such a request at such a time naturally had an effect on him, so he promised to do everything he could to make his father's family comfortable. He was not a bad young man, but rather cold-hearted, and rather selfish, although he was, in general, well respected. If he had married a pleasanter woman, he would probably have been even more respected and perhaps have become pleasanter himself, but his wife was colder and more selfish than he was.

As soon as his father was dead and buried, Mrs John Dashwood arrived unexpectedly at Norland with her child and her servants. She wished to make it clear that, as the house belonged to her husband from the moment of his father's death, she did not need any invitation from her mother-in-law. To a widow in Mrs Dashwood's situation, this appeared unforgivable. In fact, Mrs Dashwood, a sensitive and generous woman, felt so strongly about her daughter-in-law's unpleasant behaviour that she would have left the house immediately, if her eldest daughter had not begged her to reconsider.

Elinor, this eldest daughter whose advice was so useful, had a great deal of intelligence and common sense and, although only nineteen, frequently acted as her mother's adviser. To the advantage of the whole family, she was often able to persuade Mrs Dashwood to hold back the violent enthusiasms which were likely to lead them all into difficulties. Elinor had an excellent heart, full of affection, and although her feelings were strong, she knew how to control them. This was something which her mother had not yet learned to do, and which Marianne, one of her sisters, had decided never to learn.

Marianne was, like Elinor, generous, clever, and sensitive, but, unlike Elinor, she was eager in everything; her feelings were always strongly felt and expressed. In this, she was very similar to her mother. Elinor saw with concern how little her sister could control her feelings, but her mother loved Marianne for her sensibility. Now, after Mr Henry Dashwood's death, Mrs Dashwood and Marianne encouraged each other in the violence of their unhappiness, becoming more and more miserable as they remembered the past and thought bitterly of the future. Elinor, too, suffered deeply, but she could still make an effort to discuss business with her brother, be polite to her sister-in-law, and try to persuade her mother to be calmer.

The youngest sister, Margaret, was a pleasant girl of thirteen, but as she already had some of Marianne's sensibility and not much of her intelligence, she seemed likely to grow up without her sisters' advantages.

Mrs John Dashwood now made sure that everyone knew she was mistress of Norland, and that her mother-in-law and sisters-in-law were there as visitors. Her husband, however, reminded her of the promise he had given to his dying father, that he would take care of his stepmother and sisters.

'I had thought, my dear,' he added, 'of giving the girls one thousand pounds each. It would certainly be a generous present for them.'

Mrs John Dashwood did not at all approve of this. It would mean taking three thousand pounds from the fortune of their dear little boy. She begged her husband to think again. How could he rob his child, and his only child, too, of so much money? And how could the Miss Dashwoods, who were related to him only by half blood, which she considered no relation at all, possibly expect him to be so generous?

'It was my father's last request to me,' replied her husband. 'I must keep my promise to him. I must do something for them when they leave Norland for a new home.'

'Well, then, *do* something for them, but you need not give them three thousand pounds. Consider that when you have given the money, it will never come back. Your sisters will marry, and it will be gone from the family for ever.'

'You are right, my dear,' said her husband seriously.

'Perhaps I should give them half that. Five hundred pounds would be a valuable present for them.'

'Oh, beyond anything! What brother on earth would do half as much for his sisters, even if *really* his sisters! And as it is – only half blood! But you have such a generous nature!'

'I would not wish to do anything mean. It is better, on such occasions, to do too much, rather than too little. Even they themselves cannot expect more.'

'There is no knowing what *they* may expect,' said the lady, 'but the question is, what you can afford to do.'

'Certainly, and I think I can afford to give them five hundred pounds each. As it is, without my money, they will each have more than three thousand pounds on their mother's death; a very comfortable fortune for any young woman.'

'Indeed it is, and in fact I begin to think they need no extra money at all. They will be able to live very comfortably together on the interest of their ten thousand pounds.'

'That is very true, and therefore I wonder whether on the whole it would be more advisable to pay some money regularly to my stepmother during her lifetime, instead of giving money to the girls. A hundred a year would make her, and the girls while they live with her, perfectly comfortable.'

His wife hesitated a little over this plan. 'That is certainly better than giving fifteen hundred pounds all at once, but if Mrs Dashwood should live for longer than fifteen years, it would cost us more. She is very fit and healthy, and only just forty. And it is an unpleasant thing to have to pay the money out every year. One feels one's fortune is not one's own.'

'I believe you are right, my love. Whatever I can give them occasionally will be of far greater assistance than a yearly allowance, because they would only live more expensively if they felt sure of receiving a larger income. If I give them a present of fifty pounds now and then, I will, I think, be keeping my promise to my father in the fullest manner.'

'To be sure you will. Indeed, to tell the truth, I am certain your father had no idea of your giving them any money at all. The assistance he was thinking of was, I dare say, looking for a comfortable small house for them, helping them to move their furniture, and sending them occasional presents of fish and meat in season. Do consider, Mr Dashwood, how very cheaply they will live! No carriage, no horses, and only one or two servants! I cannot imagine how they will spend half their money, and it is foolish to think of giving them more. They will much more be able to give *you* something.'

'I believe you are perfectly right,' said Mr Dashwood. 'Now I understand clearly what my father meant.' And he decided to offer no more to his father's widow and daughters than such neighbourly assistance as his wife suggested.

Meanwhile, his stepmother, impatient to leave Norland, which held so many memories for her, had been looking for a suitable house to move into, not too far away. Several houses which she would have approved had already been turned down by Elinor, as too large for their income, and the search continued. Six months passed, with the two families living at Norland. Mrs Dashwood came to dislike her daughter-in-law more and more, and would have found it impossible to live in the same house with her for so long if something had not happened to make Mrs Dashwood want to keep her daughters at Norland for a while.

She had noticed a growing attachment between her eldest girl and Mrs John Dashwood's brother, a gentlemanly and pleasing young man, who had come to Norland soon after his sister's arrival, and who had spent the greater part of his time there since then. Edward Ferrars was the elder son of a man who had died very rich, but his future wealth was uncertain because the whole of his fortune depended on his mother's wishes. Neither of these facts influenced Mrs Dashwood; it was enough for her that he loved her daughter, and that Elinor returned his affection.

Edward Ferrars was not handsome, nor were his manners especially pleasing at first sight, but when he lost his shyness, his behaviour showed what an open, affectionate heart he had. His mother and sister wanted him to make a fine figure in the world in some way, but Edward was not ambitious. All his wishes were for home comforts and the quietness of private life. Fortunately he had a younger brother, Robert, who was more promising.

Mrs Dashwood completely approved of Edward, in spite of his quiet manner, which was so unlike the way she felt a young man should behave. As soon as she saw the smallest sign of love in his behaviour to Elinor, she considered their serious attachment as certain, and looked forward to their marriage in the near future.

*Mrs Dashwood had noticed a growing attachment
between Elinor and Edward.*

'In a few months, my dear Marianne,' she said, 'Elinor will be married. We shall miss her, but *she* will be happy.'

'Oh mama! How shall we manage without her?'

'My love, we shall live within a few miles of her, and see her every day. You will have a brother – a real, affectionate brother. But you look serious, Marianne. Do you disapprove of your sister's choice?'

'Perhaps I am a little surprised, mama. He is very pleasant, but there is something missing. There is no fire in his eyes. And I am afraid, mama, he has no real taste. He does not seem very interested in music, and I think he knows little of drawing or painting. And he is so calm when we discuss or read beautiful writing! It breaks my heart to hear him talk so quietly and with so little sensibility about things that matter so much to me. I could not be happy with a man who does not share all my feelings. Elinor may be happy with him, as she has not my feelings. But mama, the more I know of the world, the more I am certain I shall never see a man I can really love.'

'Remember, my love, you are not seventeen yet. It is too early in life to lose hope of happiness. Why should you be less fortunate than your mother?'

Elinor herself felt that Edward stood very high in her opinion. She believed that he also felt warmly towards her, but she was not sure enough of this to be comfortable with her sister's and mother's dreams of marriage for her. Edward sometimes appeared strangely depressed when he was with her, which worried her a little. She knew that his mother was making life difficult for him, and would perhaps disapprove of his marrying a woman with no great fortune. But sometimes she feared that he thought of her as no more than a friend.

Marianne and her mother had no such doubts, believing

strongly that any intelligent young man must love Elinor, and that love itself would solve all problems. Marianne, indeed, was quite horrified when her sister cautiously described her feelings for Edward as liking and respect, rather than love.

'Like him! Respect him!' she cried. 'Oh, cold-hearted Elinor! Why should you be ashamed of expressing love?'

Mrs John Dashwood had also noticed the attachment between her brother and Elinor. It made her uneasy, and she took the first opportunity of upsetting her mother-in-law by explaining her family's high ambitions for Edward and the importance of his marrying well, and the danger for any young woman attempting to trap him into marriage. Mrs Dashwood could not prevent herself from giving a sharp answer, and left the room at once, determined, in spite of the inconvenience, to remove herself and her daughters from Norland as soon as possible.

On the same day, she received a letter from Sir John Middleton, a gentleman who was a distant relation of hers. He wrote to offer her a small house near his home in Devonshire, where she and her girls could make their new home. Although it was only a cottage, he promised to do anything necessary to make it more comfortable. His letter was written in such a friendly way, and she was so anxious to leave Norland and her unfeeling daughter-in-law, that, after first asking Elinor's opinion, Mrs Dashwood wrote to accept Sir John Middleton's kind offer.

Chapter Two

A New Home

Mrs Dashwood took great pleasure in informing her stepson and his wife that she had found a house, and that she and her daughters would soon trouble them no longer. Mrs John Dashwood said nothing, but her husband showed some surprise.

'I do hope,' he said politely, 'that you will not be far from Norland.'

Mrs Dashwood replied, with a smile, that they were going to Devonshire. Edward Ferrars, who was in the room at the time, turned quickly towards her when he heard this.

'Devonshire!' he repeated. 'Are you really going there? So far from here! And to what part, may I ask?'

'A place called Barton, four miles north of the city of Exeter,' replied Mrs Dashwood. 'It is only a cottage, but I hope that many of my friends will come to visit me there.' She gave a very kind invitation to Mr and Mrs John Dashwood to visit her at Barton, and to Edward she gave one with even greater affection. Although her recent conversation with her daughter-in-law had made her determined to leave Norland as soon as possible, she did not in the least intend that Edward and Elinor should be separated. By giving such a clear invitation to Edward, she wished to show that her daughter-in-law's disapproval of the attachment between Edward and Elinor had not had the smallest effect.

Mr John Dashwood told his stepmother again and again how extremely sorry he was that she had taken a house so distant from Norland that he could not give her assistance in moving her furniture. He really did feel sorry, because he had decided to limit his promise to his father to this one offer of help, which would not now be of any use.

The furniture was sent to Devonshire by ship; it mainly consisted of sheets, dinner plates, books, and a handsome piano of Marianne's. Mrs John Dashwood was sorry to see the boxes leave; she felt it unnecessary for Mrs Dashwood, who had such a small income, to have any good furniture at all.

Mrs Dashwood took the house, Barton Cottage, for twelve months. It was furnished and ready for them to move into at once. All the necessary arrangements were quickly made. Elinor advised her mother to sell her carriage, which, with the horses, would cost too much to keep, and to limit the number of their servants to three. Two of the servants were sent to Devonshire immediately, to prepare the house for their mistress's arrival.

On his death bed, Henry Dashwood had told his wife of the promise his son had made, and Mrs Dashwood had never doubted that John would keep that promise. Now, as she and her daughters were about to leave Norland, was a most suitable time for him to offer them help. But Mrs Dashwood soon began to lose hope. He so frequently talked of the rising costs of managing his house and land that he seemed in need of more money himself, rather than having any intention of giving money away.

Soon they were ready to depart, and many were the tears that fell during their goodbyes to the home they loved so much. 'Dear, dear Norland!' said Marianne, walking alone in the park on their last evening. 'I shall miss you all my life!'

During the first part of their journey to Devonshire, they

were too miserable to notice anything. But when they entered Barton Valley, they became more cheerful, and began to show interest in the countryside that would soon be part of their everyday life. It was a pleasant, green valley, with thick woods and open fields. After driving for more than a mile, they reached their house.

Barton Cottage was well built and in good condition. There were two sitting-rooms downstairs, and four bedrooms and two servants' rooms upstairs. Compared with Norland, it was certainly poor and small, and the girls' tears flowed as they remembered their family home, but they soon dried their eyes and made every effort to be happy.

Mrs Dashwood was, on the whole, very pleased with the house, but she looked forward to making some changes.

'We can make ourselves quite comfortable here for the moment,' she said, 'as it is too late in the year to start any building work. To be sure, the house is rather too small for us, but perhaps next year, if I have plenty of money, as I expect I shall, we may think about enlarging the sitting-rooms, and adding a new dining-room and another bedroom. That may be easily done. It is a pity the stairs are not more handsome, but I suppose it would not be difficult to widen them. I shall see how much I have saved in the spring.'

It was not quite clear how all this work could be done from the savings of an income of five hundred a year by a woman who had never saved in her life. So, meanwhile, they were wise enough to accept the house as it was. They spent their first day arranging their things around them, to make themselves a home.

Soon after breakfast the next day, they received a visit from their landlord, the gentleman who owned Barton Cottage.

Sir John Middleton was a good-looking, cheerful man of about forty, who seemed really delighted by their arrival. He welcomed them to Barton, offering them anything from his own house and garden, Barton Park, that was lacking at the cottage. He showed a warm interest in their comfort, and hoped that they would meet his own family socially as often as possible. His kindness was not limited to words, because soon after he had left them, a large basket full of fruit and vegetables arrived from the Park, followed by another of meat and fish.

His wife, Lady Middleton, came to visit them the next day. The Dashwoods were, of course, very anxious to see a person on whom so much of their comfort at Barton must depend. Although at first they admired the elegance of her appearance and her manners, they soon realized that she did not have her husband's warmth, or anything of interest to say.

However, there was no lack of conversation, as Lady Middleton had wisely brought her eldest child with her, a fine little boy of about six. As a result, there was always something to talk about; the ladies had to ask his name and age, admire his beauty, and ask him questions which his mother answered for him. A child should be taken on every social call in order to assist conversation. In the present situation it took at least ten minutes to determine whether the boy was most like his father or mother, and why. Everybody thought differently, and everybody was astonished at the opinions of the others.

The Dashwoods would soon be given the chance to discuss the rest of the children, as Sir John had made them promise to have dinner at the Park the next day.

Barton Park was about half a mile from the cottage. It was a large, handsome house, where the Middletons lived in great comfort. Neither of them had taste, or any interest in books or music. Sir John was a sportsman, Lady Middleton a mother; he could only go shooting for half the year, while his wife was able to spoil her children all year round. He was so hospitable that they almost always had relations or friends staying in the house, but Lady Middleton's main interest lay in the elegance of her table and her domestic arrangements, of which she was extremely proud. Sir John's enjoyment of society was much more real than his wife's; he took delight in collecting about him more young people than his house would hold, and the noisier they were, the better he liked it. Barton Park was famous for its summer parties and excursions, and its winter dances.

Sir John was delighted with Mrs Dashwood and her young, pretty daughters. When they arrived at the Park that evening, he was at the door to welcome them, and repeated several times his concern that he had been unable to get any fashionable young men to meet them. There was, he said, only one gentleman there, a particular friend who was staying at the house, but who was neither very young nor very sociable. He apologized for the smallness of the party, and promised that it would never happen again. Luckily, Lady Middleton's mother had just arrived, and as she was a cheerful, pleasant woman, he hoped the young ladies would not find the evening too dull.

Mrs Jennings, his mother-in-law, was a cheerful, fat, rather vulgar old lady, who laughed and talked a great deal. During dinner she said many amusing things about lovers and husbands, and hoped the Miss Dashwoods had not left their hearts behind them in Sussex. Colonel Brandon, Sir John's particular friend, seemed as different from his friend as Mrs Jennings was from her daughter. He was silent and serious. His appearance, however, was not unpleasing, in spite of his being, in Marianne's and Margaret's opinion, an absolute old bachelor, because he was on the wrong side of thirty-five.

After dinner, Marianne was invited to sing and play the piano. Sir John was loud in his admiration at the end of every song, and as loud in his conversation with others while every song lasted. Lady Middleton frowned at him for talking, but then requested a song which Marianne had just finished. Only Colonel Brandon listened attentively, without any false show of delight. Marianne felt a respect for him that the others, with their lack of taste, did not deserve. He clearly took pleasure in music, although perhaps not with her own depth of feeling. However, she was reasonable enough to accept that a man as old as thirty-five, like the colonel, may well have outlived real feeling and true enjoyment.

Mrs Jennings was a widow, with a comfortable fortune. She had lived to see both her daughters respectably married, and now had nothing to do but to marry off the rest of the world. She spent most of her time planning weddings for all the young people she knew, and was remarkably quick at discovering attachments. Soon after her arrival at Barton, this quickness enabled her to inform the Middletons and the Dashwoods that Colonel Brandon was very much in love with Marianne. She was perfectly sure of it. It would be an excellent marriage, as *he* was rich and *she* was handsome. For a long time, Mrs Jennings had been eager to get Colonel Brandon well married, and she was always anxious to get a good husband for every pretty girl.

The immediate advantage to herself was that she could make endless jokes against them both. At the cottage she laughed at Marianne, and at the Park she laughed at the colonel. Marianne herself did not know whether to be amused or annoyed.

Marianne was invited to sing and play the piano.

'It is such a silly accusation, mama! And I think it very unfeeling of Mrs Jennings, to laugh so cruelly at old Colonel Brandon. He is old enough to be my father!'

'My dear,' said Mrs Dashwood, smiling, 'I cannot think a man five years younger than myself so extremely ancient as he appears to you.'

'But mama, really! He must have long outlived any feelings of love by now, if he ever had any when he was younger. When is a man to be safe from such cruel jokes, if age and bodily weakness cannot protect him?'

'Bodily weakness!' said Elinor. 'I know that he is older than we are, but surely you must accept that he still has the full use of his arms and legs?'

'Did you not hear him complain of having a bad back?'

'My dearest child,' said her mother, laughing, 'it must seem to you quite astonishing that *my* life has lasted to the great age of forty.'

'Mama, be serious. I know very well that Colonel Brandon is not old enough for his friends to worry yet about losing him. He may live for another twenty years. But thirty-five should have nothing to do with marriage.'

'Perhaps,' said Elinor, 'thirty-five and seventeen had better not have anything to do with marriage together. But a single woman of twenty-seven, for example, could easily consider Colonel Brandon's thirty-five years no disadvantage.'

'A woman of twenty-seven,' said Marianne, after a moment's thought, 'can never hope to feel true love again. And if her home is uncomfortable, or her fortune small, I suppose that she could accept the duties of a nurse in order to become a wife. It would be a marriage of convenience, if Colonel Brandon married such a woman. The world would be happy with it, but in my eyes it would be no marriage at all.'

'It seems a little hard,' said Elinor reasonably, 'that you consider Colonel Brandon so ill that he is in need of nursing, only because he happened to complain yesterday of a pain in his shoulder. After all, it was a cold, wet day.'

But Marianne's views remained the same. Soon after this, however, when Elinor had left the room, Marianne spoke to her mother with some urgency in her voice.

'Mama, I am anxious about Edward Ferrars. I am sure he is ill. We have now been here almost two weeks, and he still has not come to see Elinor.'

'My dear, be patient!' answered Mrs Dashwood. 'I did not expect him so soon. And I feel sure Elinor does not expect him either. When we were talking yesterday of a new fireplace for the spare bedroom, she said there was no hurry, as the room would not be needed for some time.'

'How strange! What can be the meaning of it? How cold, how calm their last goodbyes were! And Elinor is so self-controlled; she is never sad or restless or miserable. I cannot understand her.'

Chapter Three

A Handsome Stranger

The Miss Dashwoods now began to feel really at home at Barton. They went walking, and practised their drawing and music with far greater enjoyment than at any time since the death of their father. They did not have many visitors, except for those from Barton Park, as there were few other houses within walking distance. There was, in fact, a large, comfortable-looking house about a mile from the cottage, in the village of Allenham, but they heard that its owner, an old lady of good character called Mrs Smith, was unfortunately not well enough to mix in society.

There were beautiful walks all around them, in the green wooded valleys and on the hills behind the cottage. One morning, Marianne and Margaret, taking no notice of their mother's and Elinor's warnings of rain, decided to walk on one of these hills. They climbed to the top, delighted to see blue sky between the clouds, and laughing at the wind that caught at their hair and clothes.

'Nothing in the world could be better than this!' called Marianne. 'What a pity mama and Elinor did not come with us!'

But in a few minutes the blue sky disappeared, the dark clouds gathered, and driving rain began to beat down on their faces. Surprised and disappointed, they were forced to turn back. Fortunately, they were not far from home; it was just a matter of running with all possible speed down the steep side of the hill which led to their garden gate.

At first Marianne was ahead, but a false step brought her suddenly to the ground, and Margaret, unable to stop herself, carried on down the hill and through the garden gate.

A gentleman who was out shooting was walking up the hill when Marianne's accident happened. He put down his gun and ran to help her. She had hurt her ankle, and could not stand. The gentleman offered his assistance, and in spite of Marianne's protests, took her up in his arms and carried her down the hill. He took her straight into the house and placed her carefully on a sofa in the sitting-room.

He took Marianne up in his arms and carried her down the hill.

Elinor and her mother rose in astonishment as the stranger entered, carrying Marianne. While they both looked at him, secretly admiring his unusually handsome appearance, he apologized most politely for his rude entrance. Even if he had been old, ugly, and vulgar, Mrs Dashwood would have been extremely grateful to him for taking care of her child, but the influence of his looks and elegance touched her deepest feelings. She thanked him again and again, and asked the name of the person to whom she owed so much. He replied that his name was Willoughby, his present home was at Allenham, and he sincerely hoped that she would allow him to call tomorrow to enquire after Miss Dashwood. Permission was immediately given, and he then departed, to make himself still more interesting, in the middle of a heavy shower of rain.

There was general admiration of his manly beauty. Marianne had seen less of his person than the others, because of her natural confusion when he lifted her in his arms, but his appearance and behaviour seemed all that was perfect to her. Her imagination was busy, her thoughts were pleasant, and the pain of a turned ankle went unnoticed.

When Sir John next visited them, he heard all about Marianne's accident, and was eagerly asked whether he knew of any gentleman of the name of Willoughby at Allenham.

'Willoughby!' cried Sir John. 'Of course I do! He comes here every year. I shall invite him to dinner on Thursday.'

'What sort of young man is he?'

'A good man to know, I can tell you. He shoots well, and there isn't a better rider in England.'

'And is *that* all you can say for him?' cried Marianne. 'But what does he think? What are the interests close to his heart?'

Sir John looked puzzled. 'Well, I don't know as much as *that* about him. But he's pleasant, and sociable, and has got the nicest little gundog I ever saw. Did you see his dog?'

'But who is he?' asked Elinor. 'Where does he come from? Where does he live? Has he a house at Allenham?'

This time Sir John had more exact answers to give. He told them Mr Willoughby had no house of his own in Devonshire, but stayed there only while visiting the old lady, Mrs Smith, at Allenham. It appeared that he was related to her, and would inherit her fortune.

'Yes,' Sir John added to Elinor, 'he is well worth catching. He has a house and land in Somerset as well. And if I were you, I wouldn't allow my younger sister to have him, in spite of all this falling down hills. Miss Marianne must not expect to have all the men to herself. Brandon will be jealous, if she does not take care.'

'I do not believe,' said Mrs Dashwood, smiling, 'that either of *my* daughters will make any attempts at what you call *catching him*. It is not an employment to which they have been brought up. Men are very safe with us, however rich they are. I am glad to hear, however, that he is a respectable young man, whom we can meet socially.'

'I remember last Christmas,' said Sir John, 'at a little dance at the Park, he danced from eight till four without once sitting down. And he was up again at eight to go shooting.'

'Was he?' cried Marianne, with shining eyes. 'That is what I like, a young man who is enthusiastic and eager in all he does, who never gets tired.'

'I see how it will be,' said Sir John. 'You will be interested in *him* now, and never think of poor Brandon.'

Marianne's rescuer, as Margaret called him, arrived at the cottage early next morning, and was received by Mrs Dashwood with more than politeness. During his visit, Willoughby rapidly became aware of the sense, elegance, affection, and domestic comfort of the family to whom an accident had introduced him. Both Elinor and Marianne had pretty faces and lovely figures, but in Marianne's beautiful dark eyes burned an eager fire which drew Willoughby to her. She could not be silent when he spoke of music and dancing, and showed no shyness in their discussion. They soon discovered how many interests and opinions they shared, and long before his visit came to an end, they were talking and laughing together like old friends.

Willoughby visited Barton Cottage every day after that. At first, his intention was supposedly to enquire politely after Marianne's health, but soon he pretended no longer, and came to spend the whole day at her side, in complete enjoyment of her company. They read, they talked, they sang together, and Marianne found in Willoughby all the taste and sensibility which Edward Ferrars unfortunately lacked. Mrs Dashwood considered him as faultless as Marianne did. Even Elinor saw nothing wrong in him, except for the habit, which Marianne shared, of being too ready to express an opinion about other people, and of putting his personal pleasure above social correctness.

Marianne now began to realize she had been wrong to believe there was no such creature as the perfect man. Willoughby met her idea of perfection exactly, and his behaviour showed that he shared her wishes for their future. Her mother, too, had thoughts of their marriage, and secretly congratulated herself on having two such sons-in-law as Edward and Willoughby.

Elinor, however, was concerned to see that Mrs Jennings had been right, and Colonel Brandon appeared to be deeply in love with Marianne. What hope could there be for a silent man of thirty-five, against a sociable one of twenty-five? Perhaps she pitied him even more, because Willoughby and Marianne seemed determined to laugh at him for being old and dull.

'Brandon is just the kind of man,' said Willoughby one day, 'whom everybody speaks well of, and nobody cares for.'

'He is respected by all the family at the Park, however,' said Elinor sharply, 'and his conversation is always pleasant.'

'But he has nothing of interest to say!' cried Marianne.

'He has common sense, that is what I like about him. He is perfectly respectable, well informed, and, I believe, sincere.'

'Well, Miss Dashwood,' said Willoughby, laughing, 'I have three unanswerable reasons for disliking Colonel Brandon. He told me it would rain when I wanted it to be fine, he does not approve of my new carriage, and I cannot persuade him to buy my horse. So in spite of your very sensible opinion, I shall go on disliking him for ever!'

When they moved to Barton, the Dashwoods never imagined that their days would be so completely filled with parties, visits, and excursions. Sir John could not rest if there were young people to amuse, and every day there was a boat trip, or a supper party, or a drive in the countryside, or a dance at the Park. In every meeting of the kind Willoughby was included, which gave him the opportunity to develop his connection with the Dashwood family, to show his deep admiration for Marianne, and to receive, in her behaviour to himself, the clearest possible proof of her affection.

Elinor could not be surprised at their attachment. She only wished it could be less openly shown, and once or twice tried to suggest to Marianne that she should have more self-control. But Marianne, and Willoughby, too, believed that real feelings should never be hidden, and that it would be false to do so.

When Willoughby was present, Marianne had eyes for no one else.

Elinor's happiness was not as great as her sister's. In Devonshire she had found no companion who could make her forget the delights of her former home and Sussex friends. Only Colonel Brandon came closest to being the kind of friend she needed. He often fell into conversation with her, as he seemed to find some relief in talking to her about Marianne.

'Your sister, I understand, does not approve of second attachments,' he said one evening, his eyes fixed on Marianne, who was dancing with Willoughby.

'No,' replied Elinor. 'Her opinions are all romantic. She believes that we fall in love once only in our lives. But I hope that in a few years she will become more sensible.'

'That may happen. But when a romantic young mind is forced to change, what serious results there can be! I speak from experience. I knew a young lady once who—'

Here he stopped suddenly and appeared to think he had said too much. Elinor felt almost sure that his was a story of disappointed love, and her pity for him grew.

The next morning, Elinor heard a piece of news that astonished her. Marianne told her with the greatest delight that Willoughby had promised to give her a horse, so that he and she could go riding together. She had not given a moment's thought to the cost of keeping the animal, or to what society might think of her receiving such an expensive present from a young man who was not a relation. It took Elinor some time to make her understand that she could not possibly accept the gift, but finally Marianne agreed, although unwillingly.

The next day, Elinor gained a still clearer picture of Marianne's attachment to Willoughby. Margaret came excitedly to tell her that she was sure Marianne would marry Willoughby very soon.

'Oh, Elinor!' she cried. 'I have such a secret to tell you. I saw them last night after tea. Mr Willoughby was begging Marianne for something, and then he cut off a long lock of her hair, kissed it, and put it in his pocket.'

Elinor now felt sure they were engaged, and was only surprised that they had not told their relations and friends.

Sir John's latest plan for their amusement was to visit a very fine house and garden, called Whitwell, the following day. A large group of them would go in carriages, taking food and drink with them in baskets, and a most enjoyable day was expected. As Whitwell belonged to Colonel Brandon's brother-in-law, the colonel would go with them; it appeared that he alone could arrange for them to visit the house.

Unfortunately, however, while they were at breakfast at the Park, where the whole party had gathered, a letter was delivered to the colonel. He looked quickly at it, and hurried out of the room without a word. In a few moments he returned, looking more serious than usual, and explained that urgent business called him to London, and he would not, therefore, be able to join the party visiting Whitwell. He would not explain further, in spite of Mrs Jennings' insistent questioning. Everybody except Elinor tried hard to persuade him to put off his business, so that the excursion could take place, but he could not be influenced, and left the house, after wishing them a good day.

As the excursion was no longer possible, it was decided that the party would drive around the countryside instead, and the carriages were ordered. Willoughby's was first, and Marianne never looked happier than when she got into it. He drove away very fast, and they were soon out of sight. Nothing more was seen of them until their return in the afternoon.

That evening, as they all sat down to dinner, Mrs Jennings spoke quietly to Marianne, but loud enough for Elinor to hear. 'I have found you out, miss, in spite of your cleverness. I know where you spent the morning.'

Marianne blushed, and said quickly, 'Where?'

Mrs Jennings smiled knowingly. 'I hope you like your house, Miss Marianne. It is certainly very large, and when I come to see you in it, I hope you will have refurnished it. It badly needed new furniture when I was last there.'

Marianne turned away in confusion. Mrs Jennings laughed loudly, and explained that she had discovered from the servants that Marianne and Willoughby had gone to Allenham and spent a considerable time going all over Mrs Smith's house.

Elinor found this difficult to believe. Marianne had never been introduced to Mrs Smith, and it would have been very bad manners for her to enter the house while Mrs Smith was in it. However, when she asked her sister, she found that the story was true, and Marianne was quite angry with her for doubting it.

'Why should I not visit the house?' cried Marianne. 'I never spent a pleasanter morning in my life!'

'I am afraid,' replied Elinor, quietly but firmly, 'that whatever is pleasant is not always correct.'

After some minutes of serious thought, Marianne said, 'Perhaps, Elinor, you may be right. I should *not* have gone. But the rooms are lovely! There is a beautiful little sitting-room which would be delightful with modern furniture.' She would have described every room in the house if Elinor had let her.

Elinor had no time to wonder why Colonel Brandon had

been so suddenly called away. All her thoughts now centred on Marianne and Willoughby's extraordinary silence about their engagement. There seemed no reason why they should not openly tell her mother and herself, even if they did not plan to marry very soon. Willoughby was not rich; indeed, he often complained he was poor, so he might have to wait for his inheritance before marrying. But this secrecy was so opposed to their general ideas of openness and honesty that Elinor began to doubt whether they were really engaged.

Nothing could express more affection for them all than Willoughby's behaviour. He seemed to consider the cottage his home, and when Mrs Dashwood mentioned the future building work she was planning, he appeared almost horrified, and begged her not to change even one stone.

'No, Mrs Dashwood!' he cried. 'Do not spoil this house! It is perfect as it is! Remember what happiness I have known here! Promise me you will change nothing, nothing at all!'

To please him, Mrs Dashwood dutifully promised.

'I am glad of your promise. Now I would ask you one more thing. Tell me that not only your home will remain the same, but that I shall always find you and your family unchanged, and that you will always consider me with the kindness which has made you all so dear to me.'

The promise was given, and Willoughby's behaviour that evening was a proof of his happiness in their society.

Chapter Four

Departures and Arrivals

The next morning, Mrs Dashwood, with two of her daughters, went to visit Lady Middleton. Marianne wished to remain at home, and her mother, thinking that no doubt Willoughby had promised to call on her while she was alone, was quite happy to agree. When they returned from the Park, they found, as expected, Willoughby's carriage waiting outside the cottage. But what they did not expect, as they entered the house, was to see Marianne rush out of the sitting-room, sobbing uncontrollably, and run upstairs. Surprised and worried, they went into the room, where they found only Willoughby. His face showed signs of the same strong feelings that had moved Marianne.

'Is Marianne ill?' cried Mrs Dashwood.

'I hope not,' he replied, trying to look cheerful. 'Indeed, it is *I* who may expect to be ill, as I am now suffering under a very heavy disappointment. I am unable to visit you any longer. My cousin, Mrs Smith, has this morning decided to send me to London on business. As a poor dependent relation, I must do what she asks. I have already left Allenham, and now I have come to say goodbye to you.'

'This is very unfortunate. But Mrs Smith's business will not keep you from us for very long, I hope.'

He reddened as he replied, 'You are very kind, but I have no hope of returning to Devonshire immediately. My visits to Mrs Smith are never repeated within the year.'

'And is Mrs Smith your only friend? Is Allenham the only

house where you are welcome? My dear Willoughby! Surely you do not need to wait for an invitation to Barton Cottage?'

His colour deepened, and, with his eyes fixed on the ground, he only replied, 'You are too good.'

Mrs Dashwood looked at Elinor with surprise, and Elinor felt just as astonished.

After a moment's silence, Willoughby added confusedly, 'At present – my – my time is not my own… I cannot hope…' He stopped. Then, smiling weakly, he said, 'It is foolish to go on in this manner. I will not punish myself any longer by remaining among friends whose society it is impossible for me now to enjoy.' Hurriedly he said goodbye and left the house. His carriage was soon out of sight.

Mrs Dashwood's concern and alarm at his sudden departure were too great for her to express. Elinor also felt extremely disturbed by Willoughby's changed behaviour. One moment she feared that he had never had any serious intention of marrying Marianne, and the next, that some unfortunate argument had taken place between him and her sister. But her strongest feeling was one of pity for Marianne, who must now be in the depths of the most violent sorrow; and her romantic nature would consider it a duty to feed and encourage her misery.

Soon Mrs Dashwood felt able to discuss the situation with her eldest daughter. She was now more cheerful, and had persuaded herself that Willoughby was only leaving Devonshire on the orders of his rich relation, because Mrs Smith suspected, and disapproved of, his engagement to Marianne. 'His dearest wish,' she went on, 'will be to return to Barton as soon as he can.'

Elinor, listening patiently, agreed that this was quite possible.

'But if they *are* engaged,' she said, 'although it may be necessary to hide the truth from Mrs Smith, there is no reason to hide it from *us*.'

'My dear child!' cried her mother. 'It is strange for you to accuse Willoughby and Marianne of hiding their feelings, when you have accused them of showing their feelings too openly.'

*Mrs Dashwood felt able to discuss the situation
with her eldest daughter.*

'I want no proof of their affection,' said Elinor, 'but of their engagement I do.'

'I am perfectly happy with both. Has not his behaviour to Marianne, for at least the last fortnight, shown that he loved her and considered her his future wife? Is it possible, Elinor, to doubt their engagement? Willoughby must be aware of your sister's love for him. How could he leave her, perhaps for months, without telling her of his affection?'

'I confess,' said Elinor, 'that everything points towards their engagement, except for one thing – their silence on the subject – and for me that is the greatest difficulty of all.'

'Oh Elinor, I do not understand you! You prefer to believe in bad rather than good. Do you suspect Willoughby? But is he not a man of honour and feeling? You cannot really think he is deceiving Marianne?'

'I hope not, I believe not,' cried Elinor. 'I sincerely love Willoughby, and I find it painful to suspect his intentions. Perhaps, indeed, you are right, and there is a simple explanation for his strange behaviour this morning.'

They saw nothing of Marianne until dinner, when she took her place at the table without saying a word. Her eyes were red and her face pale; she avoided looking at anyone, and could neither eat nor speak. She continued in the depths of misery all evening. Any mention of anything to do with Willoughby made her burst into tears instantly, and although her family were most anxious for her comfort, it was impossible for them to keep clear of every subject which her feelings connected with him.

Marianne would have thought herself very insensitive if she had been able to sleep at all the first night after parting from Willoughby. She would have been ashamed to look her family in the face if she had not risen from her bed more in need of rest than when she lay down on it. But there was no danger of this happening. She spent most of the night sobbing bitterly, and got up with a headache. She passed the rest of the day, and several more days after that, in feeding her sorrow, by playing all Willoughby's favourite songs, by reading the books they used to read together, and by walking alone on the hills where they used to walk, until her heart was so heavy that no further sadness could be added. No letter from Willoughby came, and none seemed expected by Marianne. Her mother was surprised, and Elinor again began to worry.

One morning, about a week later, Elinor persuaded Marianne to join her sisters in a walk. As they went along the road away from the cottage, they saw a gentleman riding towards them, and at once Marianne cried out in delight, 'It is he! I know it is!'

She ran eagerly to meet him, but Elinor called out, 'Marianne, I think you are wrong. It is not Willoughby.'

But Marianne would not listen, and continued running until she was quite near the rider, when she stopped suddenly. She had realized it was not Willoughby, and her disappointment was almost too great to bear. Just then, the gentleman called to her, and she recognized Edward Ferrars.

He was the only person in the world who could at that moment be forgiven for not being Willoughby, and she smiled at him, holding back her tears. After the greetings, however, she watched with growing surprise his polite and distant behaviour to Elinor, which was very unlike a lover's. And when she heard that he had already been in Devonshire for a fortnight, without coming to see Elinor, she almost began to feel dislike for him.

'Have you been to Sussex recently?' asked Elinor.

'I was at Norland about a month ago,' replied Edward.

'How does dear, dear Norland look?' cried Marianne.

'Dear, dear Norland,' said Elinor, 'probably looks much the same as it usually does at this time of year – the woods and walks thickly covered with dead leaves.'

'Oh!' cried Marianne, 'those falling leaves gave me such delight! How I used to love seeing them driven around me by the wind! Now there is no one to watch them, no one to care.'

'It is not everyone,' said Elinor, 'who has your passion for dead leaves.'

They all returned to the cottage together, where Edward received the kindest possible welcome from Mrs Dashwood. Under her warm influence he began to lose his shyness, or coldness, and to become more like himself, but he still did not seem cheerful. This was noticed by the whole family.

'Well, Edward,' said Mrs Dashwood, after dinner, 'what are your mother's plans for you at present? Does Mrs Ferrars still want you to be a politician?'

'No, I hope my mother realizes I can never do that. I am afraid she and I will never agree in our choice of a profession for me. As you know, I did not enjoy studying law. I have always preferred the Church, but that is too ordinary for my family.'

'So how are you to become famous? Because that is what all your family wants, I understand.'

'I shall not attempt it. I have no wish to be grand or important, and I have every reason to hope I never shall be.'

'I know you are not ambitious, Edward.'

'No. I wish, like everybody else, to be perfectly happy, but in my own way. Greatness will not make me happy.'

'How right you are!' cried Marianne. 'What has wealth or

greatness to do with happiness?'

'Greatness has very little,' said Elinor, 'but wealth has much to do with it.'

'Elinor!' cried Marianne, shocked. 'Money can only give happiness where there is nothing else to give it. Beyond answering our basic needs, money is of no use to us at all.'

'Perhaps,' said Elinor, smiling, 'we may agree in the end. *Your* basic needs and *my* wealth are very much alike, I expect. Come, what is your basic figure?'

'Two thousand a year, not more than that.'

Elinor laughed. '*Two* thousand a year! *One* is my wealth! I guessed what you would say.'

'And yet two thousand a year is not a large income. A family cannot live on less. The right number of servants, a carriage, and horses for riding, cannot be paid for with less than that.'

Elinor smiled again, to hear her sister describing so accurately her future life with Willoughby.

During Edward's visit, Elinor was careful to behave to him with her usual politeness and interest, but in her heart she was alarmed by his coldness towards her. It was clear that he was unhappy, and she doubted very much whether he still loved her. She could see, however, that his feelings were confused; sometimes, for a moment, he looked at her as he used to, and this gave her hope again.

The next day, as Marianne was passing some tea to Edward, she noticed a ring on his finger, and mentioned it.

'I never saw you wear a ring before, Edward,' she cried. 'Is that your sister's hair in the ring? But surely hers is darker?'

Edward blushed deeply, and looking quickly at Elinor, said, 'Yes, it is Fanny's hair. It looks lighter than it really is.'

Elinor had met his eye, and knew the truth. She felt sure

that the hair was her own, but it must have been taken from her without her knowing. She was not in the mood, however, to disapprove of this action, and changed the subject quickly.

The Dashwoods were sorry to hear that Edward had to leave them after only a week. Although he expressed his great pleasure at seeing such old friends, and could give no good reason for his departure, there seemed to be something forcing him to leave.

Elinor blamed his mother for his rather odd behaviour. His lack of cheerfulness could easily be explained by his lack of independence. She wondered when, if ever, his mother would finally drop all her ambitions for him, and allow him to make his own choices in life. A more comforting thought was the memory of his pleasant looks and words to her during his visit, and above all, the proof of his affection that he wore round his finger.

In spite of the painfulness of Edward's departure, Elinor was determined to hide her feelings, and show a brave face to the world. Doing this did not lessen her sadness, but at least prevented her family from worrying about her. Marianne could not admire such behaviour, so unlike her own; she believed that self-control was easy for calm natures like Elinor's, and simply impossible for passionate ones like hers.

One morning soon after Edward had left, Sir John and Lady Middleton and Mrs Jennings came to visit the Dashwoods, bringing with them Mr and Mrs Palmer. Charlotte Palmer was Mrs Jennings' younger daughter, but was completely unlike her sister, Lady Middleton, in every way. She was short and rather fat, had a very pretty face, and smiled or laughed all the time. Her husband was a serious-looking young man, who made no effort to please or be pleased. He read the newspaper for most of the visit, only lifting his head from time to time to give a cross, unsmiling answer to his wife's foolish questions. She, however, took an immediate liking to Elinor and Marianne, and spent much time in conversation with Elinor in particular. When Elinor realized that their home was in Somerset, near Willoughby's, she hoped to hear more about his character, so she asked Mrs Palmer if they knew him.

'Oh yes, I know him extremely well,' replied Mrs Palmer. 'Not that I ever spoke to him, indeed, but I have often seen him in town. Everybody likes and admires him. I know very well why you ask. I am delighted that your sister is to marry him!'

'You know much more of the matter than I do,' said Elinor, surprised, 'if you have any reason to expect that.'

'Don't pretend it's not true, because you know it's what everybody in London is talking of.'

'My dear Mrs Palmer!'

'On my honour, they *all* talk of it. I met Colonel Brandon on Bond Street, and he told me of it immediately.'

'You surprise me very much. I would not expect Colonel Brandon to give such information, even if it were true.'

'Well, when I met him, I said, "Colonel, I hear there is a new family at Barton Cottage, and mama says the girls are very pretty, and that one of them is engaged to Mr Willoughby. Is it true?" And he said nothing, but from his expression I knew it was certain. Of course, I have known Colonel Brandon a long time. I believe,' she added in a low voice, 'he would have been very glad to marry me if he could. But mama did not think him a good enough husband for me. In any case, I am much happier as I am. Mr Palmer is just the kind of man I like.'

Chapter Five

Lucy Steele's Secret

The Palmers returned to Somerset the next day. But it was not long before Sir John had more visitors at Barton Park. On a morning's excursion to Exeter, he and his mother-in-law had met two young ladies, the Miss Steeles, whom Mrs Jennings discovered to be distant cousins. Sir John, always eager for society, immediately invited them to stay at the Park as soon as they were available, and, most fortunately, they were able to accept the invitation almost at once.

The young ladies arrived. Their appearance was by no means unfashionable, their dress was elegant, and their manners were very polite. They were delighted with the house and furniture, and they happened to be so madly fond of children that Lady Middleton had an excellent opinion of them by the time they had been at the Park for an hour. Sir John hurried off to Barton Cottage to tell the Miss Dashwoods.

'They are the sweetest girls in the world!' he said. Elinor smiled at this. She knew that, for Sir John, the sweetest girls in the world were in every part of England, with every possible kind of face, figure, and character. Sir John wanted the whole family to walk to the Park immediately and look at his guests. Kind, thoughtful man! It was painful to him even to keep a third cousin to himself. But in spite of his efforts, he could only gain the Dashwoods' promise to visit the Park in a day or two.

When the promised visit took place, they found nothing to admire in the appearance of the elder Miss Steele, who was nearly thirty, with a very plain face. However, the younger,

Miss Lucy Steele, who was not more than twenty-three, had a considerable beauty. Her face was pretty, she had a sharp, quick eye, and she held herself with a certain air. Elinor soon noticed the pleasing manners and constant attentions with which they were winning Lady Middleton's approval. They were full of praise for the beauty and intelligence of her children, and full of admiration for Lady Middleton herself. Fortunately for those who use these clever tricks, a fond mother can never hear enough praise of her children, and therefore will swallow anything. Lady Middleton watched proudly as her spoilt children pulled the Miss Steeles' hair, stole their sewing scissors, and tore their books; she felt no doubt that the Miss Steeles were enjoying this quite as much as her children. She was only surprised that Elinor and Marianne should sit so calmly, without taking any part in the enjoyment.

'How playful dear little William is!' she said lovingly, as her second boy violently pulled Miss Steele's finger. 'And here is my sweet Annamaria, such a quiet little thing!' She bent to kiss her daughter, but unfortunately a pin in her dress scratched the child's neck. Violent screams rang out, and the Miss Steeles rushed to help the suffering child. The little girl realized that the louder she screamed, the more attention she would receive, and nothing could be done to calm her. Finally her mother was forced to carry her upstairs, in search of her nurse, and the four young ladies were left in a quietness which the room had not known for many hours.

'Poor little creature!' said the elder Miss Steele.

'I do not think there was any real cause for alarm,' said Marianne firmly.

'What a sweet woman Lady Middleton is,' said Lucy Steele.

Marianne was silent, as it was impossible for her to say what she did not feel. It was Elinor who was forced to reply.

'She is a very fond mother,' she said, truthfully.

'And the children!' cried Lucy. 'I love to see children full of life and fun! I cannot bear them quiet.'

'I confess,' replied Elinor, 'that while I am at Barton Park, I never think of quiet children with any displeasure.'

A short silence was broken by the elder Miss Steele, who suddenly changed the subject by saying, 'How do you like Devonshire, Miss Dashwood? I suppose you were very sorry to leave Sussex. Norland is a beautiful place, is it not?'

'We have heard Sir John admire it,' said Lucy quickly.

Elinor was surprised that the Miss Steeles seemed to know so much about her family. 'Indeed, it is a lovely place.'

'And had you a great many handsome young bachelors there?' asked Anne Steele. 'I am afraid you may find it dull here. I do like a place with a lot of good-looking young men, but they must dress well and behave politely. I suppose your brother was quite an elegant young man before he married?'

'Well,' replied Elinor, 'if he was before he married, he still is, because he has not changed at all.'

'Oh dear, I never think of married men being handsome young men – they have other things to do.'

'Good heavens, Anne!' cried her sister. 'You can talk of nothing but young men – you will make Miss Dashwood believe you think of nothing else!' And she turned to another subject.

This one meeting with the Miss Steeles would have been quite enough for Elinor, who disliked the vulgar freedom and foolishness of the elder, and the clever pretences of the younger. She left the Park without wishing to know them better. The Miss Steeles, however, thought differently, and so did the sociable Sir John. Soon the young ladies of both houses were sitting or walking together for an hour or two almost every day. Anxious that they should get to know each other well, Sir John had helpfully informed the Miss Steeles of all the details of the Dashwoods' lives, and soon Anne Steele congratulated Elinor on her sister's fortunate engagement to a very fine young man.

'What a good thing to be married so young,' she added. 'I hear he is extremely handsome. I hope you may have such good luck yourself – but perhaps you have someone already.'

The Miss Steeles also heard from Sir John, with many smiles and jokes, about Elinor's suspected attachment to a young man who had recently visited Devonshire.

'His name is Ferrars,' whispered Sir John, so that everyone could hear, 'but it's a great secret.'

'Ferrars!' repeated the elder Miss Steele. 'Mr Ferrars? Your sister-in-law's brother, Miss Dashwood? A very pleasant young man. We know him very well.'

'How can you say that, Anne?' cried Lucy, who nearly always corrected everything her sister said. 'We have only seen him once or twice at my uncle's.'

Elinor was astonished. Who was this uncle? Where did he live? And how did they come to know Edward? She wished very much to have the subject continued, but nothing more was said about it, and she preferred not to ask questions herself.

In the next few days, Lucy missed no opportunity of engaging Elinor in conversation. She was naturally clever, and often amusing, and as a companion for half an hour Elinor found her quite pleasant. However, she knew nothing of books, music, or painting, in spite of her constant efforts to appear well informed. Elinor pitied her for her lack of education, but disliked her insincerity, her dishonesty, and the narrow self-interest that lay behind all her words and actions.

One day, as they were walking alone together, Lucy said, 'You will think my question strange, no doubt, but do you personally know your sister-in-law's mother, Mrs Ferrars?'

Elinor *did* think the question strange. 'I have never seen her,' she answered, a little distantly.

'Then you cannot tell me what sort of woman she is?'

'No,' replied Elinor, cautious of giving her real opinion of Edward's mother. 'I know nothing of her.'

Lucy looked fixedly at Elinor. 'I wish I could tell you – I hope you will believe I am not just being curious or impolite.' She hesitated. 'I *do* want your good opinion. And I am sure I would not have the smallest fear of trusting you; indeed I would be very glad of your advice. I am in *such* an uncomfortable situation! I am sorry you do not happen to know Mrs Ferrars.'

'I am also sorry,' said Elinor in great astonishment, 'if it could be of any use to you to know my opinion of her. But I never understood you were at all connected with that family.'

'I do not wonder at your surprise. Mrs Ferrars is nothing to me at present, but the time may come when we may be very closely connected.' She looked shyly down as she said this, with only a quick look sideways at Elinor.

'Good heavens!' cried Elinor. 'What do you mean? Connected – with Mr Robert Ferrars?' And she did not feel much delighted with the idea of such a sister-in-law.

'No,' replied Lucy, 'not with Mr *Robert* Ferrars – I never saw him in my life – but,' fixing her eyes on Elinor, 'with his elder brother, Edward.'

Elinor looked at Lucy in silent astonishment.

'You must be surprised,' continued Lucy, 'because of course

he never mentioned it to any of your family. It is a great secret, and none of my relations know of it except Anne. I would never have told *you*, if I had not trusted you completely. And I really thought I ought to explain my behaviour in asking about Mrs Ferrars. I know Mr Ferrars will not be displeased when he hears I have told you, because he has the highest opinion in the world of all your family, and looks on you and the other Miss Dashwoods quite as his own sisters.'

Elinor forced herself to speak calmly. 'May I ask how long you have been engaged?'

'We have been engaged for four years now.'

'Four years!' Elinor still felt unable to believe it.

'My sister and I often stayed at my uncle's house near Plymouth, here in Devonshire. Edward came to study law there for four years, and so we met, and became engaged. I was very unwilling to enter into it, as you may imagine, without his mother's approval, but I was too young and loved him too well to be as cautious as I ought to have been. Dear Edward! Look, I carry his picture everywhere with me.'

She took from her pocket a small painting and showed it to Elinor. Elinor's last doubts of the truth of Lucy's story disappeared as she recognized Edward's face.

'You can't think how I am suffering,' continued Lucy. 'Everything is so uncertain, and we see each other so infrequently! I wonder my heart is not broken.' Here she put a hand to her eyes, but Elinor did not feel sympathetic.

'Sometimes,' Lucy added, 'I think it would be better for both of us if I broke off the engagement completely.' She looked sharply at her companion. 'But then I cannot bear the thought of making him miserable. And to me, too, he is so very dear. What would you advise me to do, Miss Dashwood?'

'Look, I carry his picture everywhere with me.'

'I am afraid I cannot advise you in such a situation. You must decide for yourself.'

'Poor Edward! His mother must provide for him one day, but he is so depressed about his future! Did you not think him unhappy when he arrived at Barton recently?'

'Yes,' said Elinor, aware of yet another fact in support of Lucy's story.

'He had been staying with us at my uncle's. It made him so miserable, not being able to stay more than a fortnight, and seeing me so upset. He still feels just the same. I heard from him before I left Exeter.' Taking a letter from her pocket, she waved the envelope in Elinor's direction.

Elinor recognized Edward's writing, and finally had to

accept that they must be engaged. Her heart sank within her.

'Poor Edward does not even have a picture of me,' Lucy went on, 'although I have his. But I gave him a lock of my hair in a ring recently, and that was some comfort to him, he said. Perhaps you noticed the ring on his finger?'

'I did,' said Elinor. Her voice was calm, but her calmness hid an unhappiness greater than she had ever felt before. She was shocked, confused, and miserable.

Here their conversation ended, and Elinor was left alone, to think. She felt sure that Edward's affection was still hers. He certainly loved her, and had never intentionally deceived her. Unfortunately, he was now tied by an early and foolish engagement to a pretty, but insincere, vulgar, and selfish girl, whose main interest lay in his future income. Elinor's tears flowed more for Edward than herself. She had lost her chance of happiness with him, but would only be miserable for a time, while he had nothing at all to look forward to in life.

Over the next few days, Elinor took great care to hide her unhappiness. She was glad to spare her family the shocking news of Edward's secret engagement, as she knew that their affection and sorrow would only add to her misery. At convenient moments, she returned to the subject in quiet conversation with Lucy. She learned that Lucy was determined to hold Edward to the engagement, and that Lucy was jealous of her because Edward, apparently, always spoke of her with great admiration. Indeed, what other reason could Lucy have for telling Elinor her secret, if not to warn her to keep away from Edward?

Elinor realized with great sadness that Edward was not only without affection for his future wife, but that he had not even the chance of being reasonably happy in marriage.

Chapter Six

Elinor and Marianne in London

Mrs Jennings now began to make plans to return to her house in London, and quite unexpectedly invited the elder Miss Dashwoods to stay with her there.

'I've set my heart on it,' she said in her comfortable way. 'We shall have a very pleasant time together, I know, and if you do not like to go visiting with me, you can always go with one of my daughters. I have had such good luck finding husbands for my girls that I am sure your mother will think me a suitable person to look after you. If I don't get at least one of you married, it won't be my fault!'

Elinor was unwilling to accept, as she knew that her mother would miss her and Marianne very much. She was also aware that Edward and the Miss Steeles would be in London at that time, and wished to avoid meeting them. But Marianne's eagerness to see Willoughby, who would most likely be in town by then, gave Mrs Dashwood an excellent reason for insisting that they should accept Mrs Jennings' generous invitation, and so it was agreed.

During the three-day journey, Elinor had plenty of opportunity to compare Marianne's delightful expectations with her own acceptance of a cheerless future. It was clear from Marianne's bright eyes and happy smiles that she depended on finding Willoughby in London, and Elinor determined to find out more about his character and intentions.

On their arrival at Mrs Jennings' handsome house, the young ladies were given Charlotte's old room, a large and comfortable apartment. Elinor immediately sat down to write to her mother, and Marianne also sat down with pen and paper.

'*I* am writing home, Marianne,' said Elinor. 'Perhaps you should put off writing for a day or two?'

'I am *not* writing to mama,' replied Marianne quickly.

Elinor realized Marianne must be writing to Willoughby, and thought with pleasure that the fact of their corresponding must mean they were engaged.

The letters were finished, and sent to the post. During the rest of the evening, Marianne appeared very agitated. She ate almost nothing, and seemed to be anxiously listening to the sound of every carriage. Suddenly after dinner, there was a knock on the front door, and Marianne jumped up, moving eagerly towards the sitting-room door. She could not help crying, 'Oh Elinor, it is Willoughby!' and seemed almost ready to throw herself into his arms, when Colonel Brandon entered.

It was too great a shock to bear with calmness, and she immediately left the room. Elinor greeted the colonel. She was particularly sorry that a man so in love with her sister should see that Marianne felt nothing but bitter disappointment in meeting him. He was clearly astonished and concerned to see Marianne leave the room in such a way.

'Is your sister ill?' he asked anxiously.

Elinor answered unwillingly that she was, and talked of headaches, and over-tiredness, and anything that could reasonably explain her sister's behaviour. Their conversation continued on more impersonal subjects, until Mrs Jennings entered the room, with all her usual noisy cheerfulness.

'Oh Colonel!' said she, 'I am so glad to see you! And you see I have brought two young ladies with me. Your friend Miss

Marianne is here, too – you will not be sorry to hear that. I don't know what you and Mr Willoughby will do about her, between you! But Colonel, where have you been since we saw you at Barton Park? Come, let's have no secrets among friends!'

He replied politely, but gave no real answer, and did not stay long. The ladies all agreed to go to bed early.

The next morning, Marianne looked happy again. Yesterday's disappointment seemed forgotten in the cheerful expectation of what was to happen that day. They spent the morning shopping in a fashionable part of London with Mrs Palmer. During this time, Marianne was restless and inattentive, always looking out at the street, and wildly impatient to be at home again. As soon as they returned, she ran in eagerly.

'Has no letter been left for me?' she asked the servant.

'No, miss,' he replied.

'Are you quite sure? No card, or letter, or note? How very strange!' she said in a low, disappointed voice.

'Strange indeed!' Elinor thought worriedly. 'If Willoughby is in town, why does he not come, or write? Oh my dear mother, you must be wrong to permit an engagement, between a daughter so young and a man so little known, to continue in such a doubtful and mysterious manner!' For the rest of the day, Marianne seemed agitated, unable to concentrate on anything.

When they met at breakfast the next morning, Mrs Jennings said, 'If this sunny weather goes on much longer, Sir John will not want to leave Barton to come to London. It's a sad thing for a sportsman to lose a day's shooting.'

'That is true,' cried Marianne, suddenly cheerful, 'I had not thought of *that*. This fine weather will keep many sportsmen in the country. But now it is January, it cannot last. I expect we shall have frosts soon, and then they will all come to town. Why, it may even freeze tonight!'

During the next few days, Elinor was both amused and saddened to see Marianne's new-found interest in the weather. 'The wind has changed, has it not, Elinor? I feel sure it is colder than this morning. I think we shall have a frost tonight.'

Mrs Jennings was always very kind to her two young guests. Her domestic arrangements were generous, and her friends were pleasant, if a little dull. Colonel Brandon visited them almost every day; he came to look at Marianne and talk to Elinor, who saw with concern his continued affection for her sister.

About a week after their arrival, they discovered Willoughby's card on the table when they returned from their morning's drive.

'Good heavens!' cried Marianne. 'He has been here while we were out.' From this moment her mind was never quiet; the expectation of seeing him every hour of the day made her unfit for anything. She insisted on being left at home the next morning, when the others went out.

When a note was delivered the next day, she stepped quickly forward to take it. 'For me!' she cried. But it was for Mrs Jennings, and she was again disappointed.

'You are expecting a letter, then?' said Elinor, unable to keep silent any longer.

'Yes! A little – not much.' There was a short pause.

'You have no confidence in me, Marianne.'

'Elinor, how can *you* say that? You, who have confidence in no one!'

'Me!' replied Elinor in some confusion. 'Indeed, Marianne, I have nothing to tell.'

'Nor I,' answered Marianne firmly. 'So our situations are alike. Neither of us has anything to tell; you, because you communicate nothing, and I, because I hide nothing.'

And Elinor, aware that she had promised not to tell Lucy Steele's secret, felt she could not demand greater openness from Marianne than she was herself ready to offer.

The next evening was spent at a dance at Lady Middleton's London home. Once Marianne realized Willoughby was not present, she took no interest in any of the guests, and complained that she found dancing too tiring. But worse was yet to come. On their return, Mrs Jennings told them that Willoughby had been invited, and expressed her surprise that he had not appeared. Marianne looked extremely hurt, and Elinor decided to write to their mother, asking her to find out the truth from Marianne.

Elinor had only just finished her letter the next morning when Colonel Brandon arrived. Marianne, who hated visitors of any kind except one, left the room before he entered it, and Elinor found herself alone with him. He sat for a time without saying a word, and then asked her, in an agitated manner, whether he should congratulate her on gaining a brother-in-law. Elinor was not prepared for such a question, and asked him what he meant. He tried to smile as he continued, 'Your sister's engagement to Mr Willoughby is very generally known.'

'Her own family do not know it,' Elinor answered.

Surprised, he said, 'I am so sorry, I fear you may think me impolite. I had not supposed any secrecy was intended, as they openly correspond. Just now, when the servant let me in, I saw an envelope in his hand, with Mr Willoughby's address on it in your sister's writing. I came to enquire, but I am afraid I know the answer. Is it impossible for me to…? But I would have no chance of succeeding. Tell me, I beg you, that it is all arranged. Then I shall have no choice but to hide my feelings.'

'I – I am not astonished to hear of their correspondence,' replied Elinor, choosing her words carefully, 'and I am well aware of the affection they have for each other, although they have not yet informed us of the details of their engagement.'

He listened silently. 'I wish your sister all imaginable happiness, and I hope that Willoughby will try to deserve her,' he said in a voice full of feeling, and then rose to leave.

In the next few days, Willoughby neither came nor wrote. Marianne was losing hope, becoming depressed and careless of her appearance. She took no pleasure in dressing for a party she and Elinor were to attend with Lady Middleton. When they arrived in the hot, crowded room, she sank into a chair, not even looking at the other guests. Elinor, however, saw Willoughby standing nearby, in conversation with a very elegant young lady. She turned to Marianne, who noticed him at that moment. Her whole face shone with sudden delight, and she would have run to him at once, if her sister had not caught hold of her.

'Good heavens!' Marianne cried. 'He is there! Oh, why does he not look at me? Why cannot I speak to him?'

'I beg you, be calm,' said Elinor. 'Try to hide your feelings.'

But this was impossible for Marianne. She sat there, her anxiety and impatience written clearly on her face.

At last Willoughby turned round and looked at them both. Marianne jumped up and held out her hand affectionately to him. He came closer, and spoke to Elinor rather than her sister, asking in a hurried manner after Mrs Dashwood.

Marianne blushed deeply and cried, 'What is the meaning

of this, Willoughby? Will you not shake hands with me?'

He could not avoid it then, but he held her hand only for a moment. 'I did myself the honour of calling on you last week, when you were unfortunately not at home.'

'But have you not received my letters?' cried Marianne in the wildest anxiety. 'There must be some terrible mistake. Tell me, Willoughby, I beg you, what is the matter?'

'Have you not received my letters?' cried Marianne.

He looked ashamed, but, on catching the eye of the young lady with whom he had been talking, his expression seemed to harden. 'Yes,' he said, 'I had the pleasure of receiving information of your arrival in town, which you were so good as to send me,' and turned away to join his friend.

Marianne, looking horribly white, was unable to stand, and Elinor helped her to a chair. Soon Willoughby was seen to leave the party, and as Marianne was clearly unwell, Elinor asked Lady Middleton to take them home. Nothing was said between the sisters, as Marianne was suffering too much to speak. Elinor now realized that for Willoughby the attachment was over, and she felt extreme distaste for his manner of ending it.

Neither sister slept much that night, and it was still dark when Elinor was woken by the sound of agitated sobbing. She saw Marianne, only half dressed, writing as fast as a constant flow of tears would permit her.

'Marianne, may I ask—?' said Elinor gently.

'No, Elinor, ask nothing, you will soon know all.'

This was said with a sort of desperate calmness, which lasted only as long as she spoke. It seemed probable that she was writing for the last time to Willoughby.

The letter was given to a servant, to be delivered by hand, and the sisters went down to breakfast. Soon afterwards, a letter arrived for Marianne, who went deathly pale, and instantly ran out of the room. Mrs Jennings laughed comfortably.

'Is that a love letter from Willoughby? Well, well, I never saw a young woman so passionately in love in my life. I hope he won't keep her waiting much longer!'

Eager to know what Willoughby had written, Elinor hurried to their room. Marianne was lying on her bed, sobbing violently. Elinor took her sister's hand, kissed her affectionately several times, and burst into tears herself. Marianne, although unable to speak, seemed to feel her sister's loving sympathy, and silently gave her Willoughby's letter to read.

My dear madam,

I have just had the honour of receiving your letter, for which I thank you. I am concerned to find there was anything in my behaviour last night that you did not approve of, and I beg your forgiveness. I shall always remember my former visits to your family with the most grateful pleasure, but I hope I have never given anyone reason to think that I felt more for you than I ever expressed. You will accept that I could never have meant more, when you understand that my affections have long been engaged, and it will not be many weeks before the lady and I are married.

I obey your orders to return your letters, and the lock of hair which you so kindly offered me.

Your obedient servant,

John Willoughby

Elinor was horrified. She had expected a confession, explanations and reasons, but not expressed in a manner so far from every honourable and gentlemanly feeling. How could Willoughby have written a letter so cruel, so hurtful? It was a relief to her that Marianne had escaped any connection with such a man. She turned to her sister, who now felt able to speak.

'Poor Elinor! How unhappy I make you!'

'I only wish there were anything I could do which might be

of comfort to you.'

'Oh Elinor, I am so miserable!' said Marianne, before her voice was completely lost in passionate and bitter sobbing.

'Calm yourself, dear Marianne. Think of how much more you would have suffered if the discovery of his real character had come at the *end* of your engagement.'

'Engagement!' cried Marianne. 'There has been no engagement. He has not made or broken any promise to me.'

'But he told you that he loved you?'

'Yes – no – never absolutely. He never said it in so many words, but every day I read it in his eyes. I felt myself as firmly engaged as if lawyers had written the agreement for us.'

'Unfortunately, he did not feel the same.'

'He did, Elinor, for weeks and weeks he did! This lock of hair, which he says I *offered* him – he begged and begged me for it on his knees! And now – Oh! Oh!'

Elinor was quite alarmed for her sister's health, as the violence of her sobbing grew, but she managed to persuade her to take some medicine to calm her restless pain of mind and body. Kind Mrs Jennings showed real concern when she visited the patient. She had heard that Marianne's rival was a Miss Grey, a young woman with fifty thousand pounds a year, and that Willoughby had seriously overspent on his carriages and horses, and needed money urgently. Mrs Jennings had no words hard enough to describe his behaviour. She was sincerely sorry she had joked so often about Marianne's attachment, but, with a return of her natural cheerfulness, hoped that it would be all for the best, because now Marianne could marry Colonel Brandon after all.

Chapter Seven

The Truth about Willoughby

The next day, Marianne felt just as miserable, and could talk about nothing but Willoughby. With affectionate words, Elinor encouraged her to talk about her feelings. Marianne was determined to avoid Mrs Jennings' presence, however.

'She cannot feel, Elinor!' she cried. 'Her kindness is not sympathy. She is only interested in me because she will enjoy telling her friends all the details of my sad situation!'

It is unfortunate that many people of excellent intelligence and character, like Marianne, are neither reasonable nor fair. Then something happened after breakfast which sank Mrs Jennings still lower in Marianne's opinion. The sisters were in their room when Mrs Jennings hurried in, holding out a letter in her hand, and with a cheerful smile on her face.

'Now, my dear,' she cried, 'I bring you something that I am sure will do you good.'

At once Marianne imagined a letter from Willoughby, full of affection and believable explanations, instantly followed by Willoughby himself, who would throw himself passionately at her feet. The work of one moment was destroyed by the next. In front of her eyes was her mother's writing, never unwelcome till then, and in the bitterness of her disappointment she felt she had reached the depths of her suffering. She could not speak, and the tears poured down her face.

Mrs Jennings was not at all aware of what she had done, and with many kind words of sympathy, soon left the Miss Dashwoods to read the letter together. It brought them no comfort, as it expressed Mrs Dashwood's complete confidence in, and affection for, Willoughby. Marianne's tears flowed even faster when she thought how shocked and saddened her dear mother would be to hear the news. She was now very eager to return home to Devonshire. Elinor sat down, with a heavy heart, to write to her mother again, telling her how Willoughby had behaved, and asking what they should do.

Just then, there was a knock on the front door, and Marianne, looking out of the window, saw Colonel Brandon outside. She hurried away to her room, and Elinor remained to greet him. He seemed disturbed and unhappy, and asked anxiously after Marianne.

'I have come, hoping to find you alone,' he said, in some confusion, 'because... My only wish is to give comfort, no, not comfort – to support your sister in this difficult time. My feeling for her, for yourself, for your mother... Will you allow me to prove it by telling you some details of – of... If I did not consider it useful, I would not bother you...' He stopped.

'I understand you,' said Elinor. 'You have something to say about Mr Willoughby, that will open his character to us. Telling me would be the greatest proof of friendly feeling for Marianne. I beg you, let me hear it immediately.'

'I must tell you a little about myself first. Perhaps you remember at Barton Park, when I mentioned a young lady I once knew? She was very like your sister, with an eager mind, a warm heart and great sensibility. She was a distant cousin of mine, and from our earliest days we played together and loved each other. But at seventeen she was married, against her wishes, to my brother. Just before the wedding, she and I planned to run away and get married secretly, but my father discovered the plan, and sent me away to join the army. It was an extremely unhappy marriage. My brother did not love or respect her, and spent his time on pleasures most unsuitable for a husband. She was very young, had no friends or family to advise her (I had been sent abroad by then), and my brother's bad example was always with her. I cannot describe the shock I received when I heard, two years later, of her divorce...'

He could not speak for a moment, and when he saw Elinor's concern and sympathy, took her hand and kissed it gratefully.

'When I returned to England three years later, I began to search for her, but she was no longer with her first seducer, the man for whom she had left her marriage. There was every reason to fear she had left him only to sink deeper into a life of dishonour. After six months, however, I *did* find her, in a debtors' prison. She was so changed, so thin, so ill! She had only a short while to live, so I made sure she was properly looked after, and I was with her in her last moments.'

He stopped for a moment to control himself, then went on. 'With a firmer mind, and a happier marriage, she could have been everything you will live to see in your sister. She left to my care her little girl, Eliza, the child of her first seducer. I sent Eliza to school, and then put her in the care of a very respectable woman living in the country. She is now seventeen. Imagine my horror when she suddenly disappeared a year ago! For eight long months I searched, and found nothing. You can imagine what I thought, and feared, and how I suffered.'

'Good heavens!' cried Elinor. 'Could Willoughby—'

'The first news of Eliza came in the letter I received at Barton Park, on the morning of our planned excursion to Whitwell. That was why I left so suddenly. Willoughby did not know that I was called away to help someone *he* had made poor and miserable. But if he had known, would he have cared? No! He had done what no man of feeling would do. He had left the girl whose innocence he had seduced – left her with no home, no friends, and no money.'

'This is beyond everything!' cried Elinor.

'Now you understand what he is like. Imagine what I have felt all these weeks, knowing his character, and seeing your sister as fond of him as ever. Who can tell what his intentions were towards your sister? One day, she will doubtless feel grateful, when she compares her situation with that of my poor Eliza. At least there is no dishonour in your sister's suffering, and every friend of hers must feel concern for her unhappiness, and respect for her bravery in bearing it.'

Elinor thanked the colonel warmly for his kind words. 'Have you,' she continued, 'seen Willoughby since you left Barton?'

'Yes. Once,' he replied seriously. 'As Eliza had confessed to me the name of her seducer, I accused him of dishonourable behaviour and challenged him to a duel. We met by appointment, but both of us returned unwounded. And my poor Eliza has had the child she was expecting, and now remains in the country.'

After this, the colonel left, and Elinor very soon passed on the details of the conversation to her sister. The effect was not quite what she had hoped. Marianne listened attentively, and appeared to accept Willoughby's guilt. She no longer avoided the colonel when he came to the house, and talked to him in a gentle, pitying voice. But she seemed even more depressed, now that Willoughby's good character had been lost, as well as his heart.

Mrs Dashwood's letter of reply arrived next day. Her disappointment was almost more painful than Marianne's, and her anger even greater than Elinor's. But she advised them not to shorten their stay with Mrs Jennings, which had been expected to last five or six weeks, as a speedy return to Barton would only remind Marianne of former happy times with Willoughby. She also hoped that Elinor would see more of the Ferrars family, who would soon be arriving in London.

Sir John, Mrs Jennings, and Mrs Palmer all spoke forcefully about Willoughby, and determined to have nothing to do with him ever again. They talked so much about him, however, that it was a happy relief to Elinor when Lady Middleton showed only calm and polite unconcern. Whenever the subject was discussed she would say gently, 'It is very shocking indeed!', but privately she was already planning to visit Mrs Willoughby, who would be a woman of elegance and fortune.

Mrs Jennings was disappointed to see that the colonel did not look more cheerful now that he no longer had a rival for Marianne. There seemed to be a better understanding between the elder Miss Dashwood and the colonel, and Mrs Jennings, who had quite forgotten Edward Ferrars, began to think that *Elinor* would become Mrs Brandon.

A fortnight after Willoughby's letter had arrived, Elinor had the painful duty of informing Marianne that he was married. Marianne received the news bravely at first and said nothing; but the tears came later, as wildly and as passionately as before.

About this time, Elinor was sorry to see the Miss Steeles arrive in London, as their presence always gave her pain. Lucy pretended to feel great delight in finding them in town, and Elinor had to use all her self-control to answer politely.

A pleasanter meeting took place a little later, when their brother, John Dashwood, came to visit them at Mrs Jennings'. He enquired after their health and their mother's, and was introduced to Colonel Brandon, who happened to be there. As it was a fine day, he asked Elinor to take a short walk with him. As soon as they were out of the house, his questions began.

'Who is Colonel Brandon? Is he a man of fortune?'

'Yes, he has a large house with some land, and, I believe, about two thousand pounds a year.'

'I think, Elinor, I will soon be congratulating you on making a very respectable marriage. He seems most gentlemanly, and he likes you, I am sure of it.'

'He has not the smallest wish to marry *me*.'

'You are wrong, Elinor. A very little effort on your side will catch him. Some of those little encouragements, which ladies can so easily give, will fix him, in spite of the smallness of your fortune. You should try for him. How amusing if Fanny had a brother, and I had a sister, marrying at the same time!'

'Is Mr Edward Ferrars,' Elinor said calmly, 'going to marry?'

'It is not actually arranged yet, but the lady is Miss Morton, Lord Morton's only daughter, with thirty thousand pounds of her own. Edward's mother will most generously allow him a thousand a year, if he marries Miss Morton. I wish *we* could live so comfortably. I am afraid our income is not large enough for us to live as we would like.' And he shook his head sadly at the thought of his own difficulties.

The following week, Mr and Mrs John Dashwood gave a grand dinner party. The Middletons, Mrs Jennings, Colonel Brandon, the Miss Dashwoods, and the Miss Steeles were all invited. Elinor and Lucy both knew that Mrs Ferrars would be present as well.

'Pity me, dear Miss Dashwood!' whispered Lucy, as they walked up the stairs. 'In a moment I shall see the person on whom all my happiness depends – my future mother-in-law!'

Mrs Ferrars was a little, thin woman, with a disagreeable expression. She was not a woman of many words, but she made it very clear that she strongly disliked Elinor, and as strongly approved of Lucy.

'If she knew Lucy's secret,' thought Elinor, amused, 'how she would hate her!' She felt almost relieved that she could not now hope to become Edward's wife, with such a mother-in-law.

The next morning, Elinor received a visit from Lucy, who had been so delighted by Mrs Ferrars' welcoming behaviour to her that she felt she simply had to tell her dear friend about it.

'She was *so* kind to me! Did you not notice it? And your sister-in-law, too! What elegant, delightful women they are!'

Before Elinor could bring herself to reply, the door opened and Edward walked in. It was a very difficult moment for the three of them, but Elinor took control of the situation. Anxious to show that nothing was wrong, she welcomed him in her usual way. Lucy kept silent, watching Elinor narrowly out of the corner of her eye, while Edward did not know what to say, in his confusion, and could not keep the conversation going. Soon Elinor decided bravely to leave the engaged couple alone for a while, and went to fetch Marianne.

Rushing delightedly into the room, Marianne cried, 'Dear Edward! This is a moment of great happiness!' and looked lovingly at him and her sister. There was a short silence.

'My dear Edward!' Marianne continued. 'Why did you not come last night, to your sister's dinner party? We were all there.'

'I had – an appointment – somewhere else.'

'An appointment! But was that so important, when such friends wanted to see you?'

'Perhaps, Miss Marianne,' said Lucy smoothly, 'you think

young men never keep their appointments or their promises.'

Elinor was very angry, but Marianne just answered, 'No, I trust Edward. He is the most thoughtful, unselfish person I have ever met. He would never knowingly hurt anyone, I know.'

This praise was so unacceptable to Edward that he very soon got up to leave, and Elinor had every reason to expect that this painful meeting would not be repeated.

John and Fanny Dashwood continued to see Elinor and Marianne at London parties and dances, and John began to wonder about inviting his sisters to stay for a few days.

Fanny, however, was astonished at this suggestion. 'My love, I would ask them with all my heart if it was possible. But I had just decided to ask the Miss Steeles to stay with us. We can ask your sisters some other year, you know.'

Mr Dashwood agreed at once, and Fanny, delighting in her escape, and proud of her quick thinking, wrote to invite Lucy and her sister. This made Lucy really happy. Such an opportunity of being near Edward and his family was the most useful thing in the world for her. And when the invitation was shown to Elinor, she began for the first time to share Lucy's expectations, and prepared herself to hear officially of the engagement.

Chapter Eight

Edward's Engagement

Mrs Jennings was very busy at this time, as her daughter Charlotte had just had a baby and was clearly in need of a fond mother's advice. She visited Charlotte at least twice a day, and it was at the Palmers' house that she heard a most interesting piece of news. She hurried excitedly back to tell Elinor.

'My dear Miss Dashwood, have you heard? Your sister-in-law is ill! Charlotte's doctor told me! And do you know why? It appears that Edward Ferrars, the young man I used to joke with you about, has been engaged for over a year to Lucy Steele! And no one knew a word of the matter except her sister Anne! Could you have believed such a thing possible? What happened was this: the Miss Steeles are staying with your brother and his wife, as you know. Anne, who is a kind creature but of no great intelligence, thought that there would be no difficulty, as Fanny Dashwood seemed to like Lucy so much, so she told her all about the engagement. Well, your sister-in-law fell on to the floor, and started sobbing and screaming so violently that your brother had to send for the doctor. Lucy and Anne were told to pack their bags and leave at once. Of course, the Ferrars family wanted Edward to marry that rich Miss Morton. But I have no pity for them. I cannot bear people who think money or greatness is important. There is no reason why Edward should not marry Lucy. She knows better than anyone how to make the most of everything, and if Edward's mother allowed him five hundred pounds a year, they could live comfortably.'

Mrs Jennings, to Elinor's relief, no longer suspected her of having any interest in Edward, but she could talk of nothing else. Elinor, knowing that Marianne would be fierce in her anger against Edward, was now anxious to tell her sister the truth and to prepare her to hear the subject discussed.

Marianne listened to Elinor's story with horror, and cried without stopping. For some time, Edward seemed a second Willoughby to her. She could not understand his behaviour, or accept that he could feel affection for such a person as Lucy.

'How long have you known this, Elinor?' she asked.

'Four months. Lucy told me of her engagement at Barton, and I promised to keep it secret.'

'What! All the time you were looking after me in my misery, this has been on your heart? How could you bear it?'

'By feeling that I was doing my duty. I had to keep Lucy's secret, and I did not want to worry my family and friends.'

'Four months! And yet you loved him!'

'Yes. But I loved my family, too, and I was glad to spare them the sorrow of knowing how I felt. Now I no longer feel unhappy. I do not consider Edward has behaved badly in any way, and I wish him every happiness. He will always do his duty, and Lucy does not lack sense. They will marry, and time will teach him to forget that he ever thought another woman better than *her*.'

'If such is your way of thinking, your self-control is perhaps a little less to be wondered at. I understand it better.'

'I know you do not suppose I have ever felt much, but, Marianne, for four months I have had all this on my mind, and been unable to speak of it to a single creature. I was told about it by the person whose early engagement destroyed my hopes of happiness. She saw me as a rival, and was delighted to see me defeated. I have had to listen to her talking about

Edward again and again; I have had to pretend to show no interest in him; I have had to bear the unkindness of his sister and the rudeness of his mother – without enjoying any of the advantages of an attachment to him. I know now that I shall be divided from Edward for ever. If you can ever think me capable of feeling, Marianne, surely you may suppose that I have suffered *now*.'

These words went straight to Marianne's heart. 'Oh, Elinor!' she cried. 'You have made me hate myself for ever. How unkind I have been to you, you who have been my only comfort!' And the two sisters fell sobbing into each other's arms.

Marianne was so sorry she had misjudged her sister that she promised to do anything Elinor wanted – to discuss the engagement in public without bitterness, to meet Lucy without showing any dislike, and even to talk to Edward himself, if chance brought them together, with her usual friendliness.

The next morning brought a test of her self-control, when John Dashwood came to visit Mrs Jennings and his sisters.

'You have heard, I suppose,' said he, with a most serious expression, 'of our very shocking discovery yesterday.'

Silently, they all showed that they had; it seemed too awful a moment to speak.

'Your sister-in-law,' he continued, 'has suffered terribly. So, too, has Mrs Ferrars. But I would not alarm you too greatly. The doctor says Fanny is strong, and will get better, in time. She says she will never think well of anybody again. And I cannot wonder at it, as she was so deceived! How ungrateful those young women were, after she had shown them so much kindness! "I wish with all my heart," says poor Fanny in her affectionate way, "that we had invited your sisters instead of them."'

Here he stopped to be thanked; then continued.

'What poor Mrs Ferrars suffered cannot be described. She could not believe Edward was secretly engaged, when all the time she had been planning a most excellent marriage for him. She sent for him, and he came to see her. I am sorry to tell you what happened next. All our attempts to persuade Edward to end the attachment were useless. Even when his mother explained that if he married Miss Morton, she would generously allow him a thousand pounds a year, and even when she offered to make it twelve hundred pounds, he still insisted that he would not break the engagement. Mrs Ferrars then told him he would receive no money at all from her, and if he entered any profession, she would do her best to prevent him succeeding in it.'

'Good heavens!' cried Marianne. 'Can this be possible!'

'Your surprise is very natural, Marianne,' said her brother. 'It is astonishing that Edward could not be persuaded.'

Marianne, about to disagree fiercely, remembered her promises to Elinor, and said nothing.

'Well,' cried Mrs Jennings, 'I think he has behaved like an honest man. He must keep his promise to marry Lucy Steele. If he broke it, the world would think him a worthless scoundrel.'

'I respect your views, madam,' said John Dashwood politely, 'but I am afraid that a good, thoughtful mother like Mrs Ferrars, with such a very large fortune, cannot approve of her son's secret engagement to this most unsuitable young woman. I am sorry to say that it has all ended in a most unhappy separation. Mrs Ferrars told Edward to leave her house, and he obeyed at once. She does not wish to see him ever again, and has now decided, very understandably, that Robert, not Edward, should inherit her fortune when she dies. Poor

Edward! His younger brother will be wealthy while he remains poor. I feel for him sincerely.'

John Dashwood left soon afterwards, and the three ladies immediately joined together in their firm disapproval of Mrs Ferrars' behaviour and their warm praise of Edward's.

The next morning, Elinor received a letter from Lucy.

I hope, my dear Miss Dashwood, you will not mind my writing to you. I know that, as a true friend, you will be pleased to hear my news. Edward and I, although we have suffered terribly in all our recent troubles, are quite well now, thank God, and happy in each other's love. We are very grateful to our friends, yourself not the least among them, for helping us through our many difficulties. I shall always remember your great kindness, and so will Edward. I am sure you will be glad to hear that I spent two happy hours with him yesterday. I offered him his freedom, and was ready to consider our engagement at an end, if that was what he wanted. But he would not hear of it, and said he did not care about his mother's anger, as long as he had my affections. Life will not be easy for us, it is true, but we must wait, and hope for the best. He will enter the Church soon, and if you ever have the opportunity to recommend him to anybody who can give him a living, I am sure you will not forget us. And dear Mrs Jennings, too – I hope she will say a good word for us to any friend who may be able to help us. I beg you to remember me to her, most gratefully and respectfully, and to Sir John and Lady Middleton, and the dear children, and give my love to Miss Marianne.

Yours truly, Lucy Steele

Elinor felt sure that Lucy wanted the letter to be seen by Mrs Jennings, and showed it to her immediately.

Mrs Jennings was full of praise for Lucy's warm heart. 'How prettily she writes!' she said. 'She calls me dear Mrs Jennings, you see. I wish I *could* get him a living, with all my heart.'

The Miss Dashwoods had now been in London for more than two months, and Marianne was becoming more and more impatient to go home. She missed the air, the freedom, the quiet of the country. Elinor, although almost as anxious to leave as her sister, was aware of the difficulties of a long journey. This problem appeared to be solved when the Palmers invited Mrs Jennings and the Miss Dashwoods to their home in Somerset, only a day's journey away from Barton. They planned to travel there at the end of March. The invitation was gladly accepted; Elinor and Marianne would stay a week with the Palmers, and then continue their journey to Barton.

Soon after this arrangement had been made, Colonel Brandon called at Mrs Jennings' house and was told the news.

'My dear colonel, I do not know what you and I will do without the Miss Dashwoods,' said Mrs Jennings. 'How lonely and dull we shall be!'

She hoped these words, and the sad picture they painted, would persuade him to make the offer of marriage which might prevent any loneliness or dullness in the future. And with delight, she saw that her plan had succeeded. When Elinor moved to a quiet corner of the room, Colonel Brandon joined her there, and talked very seriously to her for several minutes. Although Mrs Jennings was too honourable to listen, she could not help seeing that Elinor was blushing and looking agitated. Some of the colonel's words reached Mrs Jennings' ears, and astonished her greatly. '*I do apologize for the smallness of the house.*' What could he mean? She knew very well that there were fifteen bedrooms and five sitting-rooms in his house at Delaford. '*I am afraid it cannot happen soon.*' What an unlover-like thing to say! There could be no reason at all to delay their marriage.

In fact, the colonel was talking on a quite different subject. He had heard of Edward's difficulties, and, knowing him to be a friend of Elinor's, wished to help the young man. A living at Delaford had just become vacant, and the colonel was asking Elinor to offer it to Edward.

'At least it would be a start for Mr Ferrars. The vicar's duties there are light, and there is a cottage that goes with the post, although I do apologize for the smallness of the house. The income is only two hundred pounds a year, so I am afraid his marriage cannot happen very soon.'

Elinor expressed her grateful thanks for the colonel's generous offer, and promised to tell Edward the good news.

Some of the colonel's words reached Mrs Jennings' ears.

When Colonel Brandon had left, Mrs Jennings spoke to Elinor with a knowing smile. 'Well, Miss Dashwood, I couldn't help overhearing the colonel's words, and I can tell you, I was never better pleased in my life!'

'Yes,' said Elinor, 'it *is* a matter of great happiness to me. But I was so surprised when he spoke to me about it!'

'My dear, I'm not in the least astonished by it. I wish you every happiness, and if I want to see a happy couple, I know where to look for them in future!'

'At Delaford, I suppose,' said Elinor with a smile.

'That's right, my dear. And I can tell you, you won't find the house small! Now, I must go out, but we'll continue our conversation later. I'm sure you want to tell your sister about it.'

'Certainly, madam, but I shall not mention it to anyone else at present.'

'Oh,' said Mrs Jennings, disappointed. 'Then you would prefer me not to tell Charlotte, or Sir John, or Lucy.'

'Yes, madam, if you don't mind. I must speak to Mr Ferrars first, to arrange matters with him.'

This was, at first, extremely puzzling for Mrs Jennings, but after a moment's thought she had a happy idea. Edward must be the vicar they had chosen to carry out the wedding ceremony! She hurried excitedly off on her morning visits, aware of the important secret that she was not allowed to tell. By chance, as she left the house, she met Edward at the door. He had called only to leave a note, but Mrs Jennings insisted on his going in to see Miss Dashwood, who had particular news to give him.

Elinor had begun to write a letter to Edward when she looked up to find him standing in front of her. Her astonishment and confusion were very great. Edward, too, was confused, and for a few moments neither knew what to say to the other. At last, however, the colonel's offer was made, and Edward, although astonished at this kindness from a stranger, was deeply grateful for the opportunity. He soon realized that he owed more than he could express to Elinor, and also began to suspect that the colonel might have a particular reason for wishing to help any friend of hers. There was sadness in his eyes as he rose to say goodbye.

'When I see him again,' said Elinor to herself, as the door shut behind him, 'I shall see him the husband of Lucy.'

When Mrs Jennings returned, she was eager to find out more. 'Well, my dear, and how soon will the young man be ready?'

'In two or three months, I imagine,' replied Elinor.

'Two or three months! My dear, how calmly you talk! Can the colonel wait so long? I know you wish to do a kindness to Mr Ferrars, but could you not find someone who is already a vicar?'

'My dear madam, what can you be thinking of? The colonel's only intention is to be of use to Mr Ferrars.'

'Good heavens, my dear! Surely you do not mean that the colonel only marries you in order to give ten pounds to Mr Ferrars as his vicar's fee for the ceremony!'

The confusion could not continue after this, and there was much amusement as Elinor explained. Mrs Jennings was just as delighted with the true situation, and looked forward to visiting Lucy and Edward in the vicar's house at Delaford in a few months' time. Elinor now knew that Edward's marriage to Lucy was certain; she herself had helped to smooth the path towards it.

Chapter Nine

Marianne's Illness

Before leaving London, Elinor paid one last visit to her brother and his wife. Fanny did not wish to see her, and stayed in her room, but John was very interested in the news of Edward's good luck. He could not understand why the colonel should give away a living, when he could have sold it. But he had something more particular to say to his sister. Taking her hand, he spoke in a very serious whisper.

'There is one thing I must say, because I know it will please you. I know, in fact, Fanny heard her mother say, that although perhaps she did not approve of… of a certain attachment of Edward's – you understand me – it would have been far preferable to her than *this* engagement to Miss Steele. Of course all that is quite in the past now, and out of the question. But I thought I would just tell you, my dear Elinor. Not that you have any reason to be sad. There is no doubt of your doing extremely well. Has Colonel Brandon been with you lately?'

Elinor was glad to be spared the need to reply by the entrance of Mr Robert Ferrars. She had only met him once before and had found him a thoughtless and insensitive young man, full of his own self-importance. This short meeting only served to support her low opinion of his head and heart. He talked happily of Edward's inheritance, which *he* would now enjoy, and laughed loudly at the idea of Edward as a poor vicar living in a cottage.

'His engagement certainly was very shocking news,' he added. 'I said to my mother, "My dear madam, I do not know what *you* intend to do, but for myself, I must say that if Edward marries this young woman, *I* shall never see him again." I saw the girl once, you know, just a plain, country girl, with no elegance or beauty. I cannot help thinking that if I had heard of the connection earlier, I could have persuaded Edward to break it off. But now it is all too late. He must be punished, that is certain.'

Elinor was relieved that she could not stay long, and sincerely hoped she would not see Robert Ferrars again.

The journey to Cleveland, the Palmers' home in Somerset, took two days. Their house was comfortable and modern, with large, well-kept gardens and woods. On her arrival, Marianne went straight into the garden. She was feeling more agitated than usual, aware of being only eighty miles from Barton and only thirty from Willoughby's country house, but she loved being back in the romantic countryside. She determined to spend as much time as possible taking lonely walks through the gardens and woods. Alone, she would be free to delight in her misery, thinking, dreaming, remembering.

The hours passed quietly at Cleveland. Mrs Palmer had her child, and Mrs Jennings her sewing. Elinor was surprised to find Mr Palmer very capable of being a pleasant companion, and only occasionally rude to his wife and mother-in-law. Colonel Brandon, who was also a guest of the Palmers', spent a great deal of time with Elinor, talking to her about the vicar's house at Delaford and the repairs he was planning to have done to it. His pleasure in her conversation and his respect for her opinion would have been enough to justify Mrs Jennings' view of his attachment, and even, perhaps, to make Elinor suspect it herself. She still felt certain, however, that while he spoke to *her*, it was Marianne at whom he looked, and of whom he thought. When Marianne mentioned that she had a sore throat, and felt unwell, the colonel appeared extremely worried. In his concern Elinor saw the quick feelings and needless alarm of a lover.

Two delightful evening walks in thick wet grass had given Marianne a violent cold. She felt heavy and feverish, with pains all over her body, but at first refused all medicines, saying that a good night's rest was all that she needed.

The next day, however, she was worse, unable to do anything except lie miserably on a sofa, and after another restless, feverish night, Elinor was very ready to send for the Palmers' doctor. After examining his patient, he said that she was suffering from an infection, and would recover in a few days. But the word 'infection' greatly alarmed Mrs Palmer, who feared that her baby might catch it, and she persuaded her husband to take her and the child to stay with a near relation, until there was no further danger of illness at Cleveland. Mrs Jennings kindly insisted on staying with the Miss Dashwoods, as she felt responsible for the young ladies in their mother's absence, and Colonel Brandon also offered to stay, in case a gentleman's help was needed. Poor Marianne now felt really ill, and extremely miserable, as their return to Barton would have to be considerably delayed.

Several days passed, and Marianne's condition remained the same. The doctor came every day, talking each time of a speedy recovery, and Elinor was just as hopeful. In her letters home, she had not told her mother of the seriousness of Marianne's illness, and now congratulated herself on not alarming Mrs Dashwood unnecessarily. But that evening, Marianne became restless again, and Elinor stayed beside her bed, watching her turning feverishly from side to side. Suddenly Marianne sat up and cried wildly, 'Is mama coming?'

'Not yet,' replied Elinor, hiding her terror, and helping her sister to lie down again. 'It is a long way from Barton.'

'But she must come soon!' cried Marianne desperately. 'I shall never see her again if she does not come soon!'

Marianne's condition remained the same.

Elinor was so alarmed that she sent for the doctor at once, and decided to send a messenger to Barton to fetch her mother. She spoke immediately to Colonel Brandon, who, although greatly depressed and fearing the worst, was ready to help in any way, and offered to drive to Barton himself. How grateful Elinor was for the comfort of such a friend as the colonel at that moment! Not a second was lost in delay of any kind, and the colonel drove off into the night, leaving Elinor to watch over her sister.

Both sisters suffered greatly during that night, Marianne in her sleepless pain and fever, and Elinor in cruel anxiety that her mother would arrive too late to see her dear child alive. When the doctor came, he had to confess that his medicines had failed, and that the infection was stronger than ever. Elinor was calm, except when she thought of her mother, but she was almost without hope. She stayed by her sister's bed all morning, her thoughts confused and sorrowful.

But at midday, she began to see signs of the fever going down. Cautiously, she told herself not to hope, but soon it seemed almost certain, and on the doctor's next visit, he was able to congratulate her on Marianne's slow but sure recovery. Mrs Jennings showed her delight by talking and laughing without stopping, but Elinor's feelings were of a different kind. Her relief and happiness were strong, but silent. That evening, Marianne fell into a quiet, comfortable sleep, and Elinor knew that at last she was out of danger.

Her thoughts now began to turn to her mother's arrival, which was expected at any moment. Mrs Jennings persuaded her to leave Marianne's bedside for a few minutes to drink some tea, but Elinor soon returned, to sit by her sleeping sister and wait for the travellers from Barton. The night was cold and stormy, but as long as Marianne slept peacefully, Elinor did not mind the beating of the rain on the windows, or the noise of the wind blowing round the house.

At eight o'clock, she heard a carriage drive up to the front door. Knowing what her poor mother must be feeling, Elinor found it impossible to be calm, and hurried downstairs. She rushed into the sitting- room, and saw – Willoughby.

With a look of horror, she stepped backwards, and was about to leave the room, when he said rapidly, 'Miss Dashwood, I beg you to stay. I have something I must tell you.'

Elinor was astonished. 'To tell *me*? Well, sir, if you must. But be quick. I have no time to spare.'

'Tell me first, is your sister really out of danger?'

'We hope she is,' replied Elinor coldly.

'Thank God! I heard she was ill, and I have driven all day to get here. I have come to offer some kind of explanation, to show you that I have not always been a scoundrel, and to receive something like forgiveness from Ma— your sister.'

'Marianne has already forgiven you.'

'Has she?' he cried eagerly. 'But listen, I must explain. When I first met your family, I had no other intention than to pass the time pleasantly while in Devonshire. My income was never large, and my debts are always very great, so I was planning to attach myself to a woman of fortune. But I soon found myself sincerely fond of your sister, and the happiest hours of my life were spent with her. I allowed myself, most wrongly, to put off asking her to marry me. At last I determined to speak of marriage, but unfortunately my relation, Mrs Smith, had just discovered a connection' – he reddened, and looked away – 'but you have probably heard the whole story from Colonel Brandon.'

'I have,' replied Elinor, also blushing, 'and I cannot see how you will explain away your part in that terrible business.'

'No, I know I was at fault,' cried Willoughby, 'but I must ask you to believe that I had no idea Eliza was in such need. *I* suffered, too, because Mrs Smith was extremely angry at my behaviour, and refused to allow me any more money, or see me again. I knew that if I married Marianne, I would be poor, and I couldn't bear the thought of that. So I came to Barton Cottage, to say goodbye to her. How happy I had been, the day before, ready to become engaged to her! And how miserable I was when I saw her sorrow and deep disappointment! Oh God! What a hard-hearted scoundrel I was!'

There was a short silence, while Willoughby recovered his self-control, and Elinor's heart softened a little towards him.

'And then in London, Marianne's notes to me! Every word was a knife in my heart! She was far dearer to me than any other woman in the world, but by then I was engaged to Miss Grey!'

'Do not speak like that of my sister, Mr Willoughby,' said Elinor. 'Remember that you are a married man now.'

He began to laugh wildly. 'Married, yes. Did you like the letter I wrote to Marianne? Miss Grey happened to see Marianne's last note to me, and read it. Her jealous anger made her think of a cruel punishment for me. She told me what to write, and watched over me as I wrote the letter. They were all her own gentle words, her own sweet thoughts. I could not risk losing her – I needed her money to pay my debts.'

'You ought not to speak of Mrs Willoughby in this way. You have made your choice, and should respect your wife.'

'She does not deserve your pity. I have no chance of domestic happiness with her. But do you think me less guilty than before? Will you tell your sister, when she is recovered, what I have told you? If ever, one day, by some happy chance, I were free again—' Elinor stopped him with a frown. 'Well, I shall leave now. I shall live in terror of one event – your sister's marriage.'

'She can never be more lost to you than she is now.'

'But someone else will have her. And if that someone were he, whom of all men I could least bear... But I must go. Goodbye.' And he almost ran out of the room.

Elinor's heart was full as she returned to her sleeping sister. The past, the present, the future – Willoughby's visit and the pity she felt for him, Marianne's health and her mother's expected arrival, made her so agitated that she did not notice her hunger or tiredness. Only half an hour later, a second carriage arrived at the house. Elinor hurried to the door, just in time to receive and support her mother as she entered, half-dead with fear. In a moment, Elinor was able to give the good news, and Mrs Dashwood's tears silently expressed her relief. Colonel Brandon shared her feelings in an even greater silence. In two minutes, Mrs Dashwood was with her suffering child, made dearer than ever by absence, unhappiness, and danger.

Marianne's recovery continued every day, and Mrs Dashwood soon found an opportunity to tell Elinor another piece of news. On the long drive from Barton to Cleveland, Colonel Brandon had been unable to hide his feelings, and had told Mrs Dashwood that he had long wanted to marry Marianne. Mrs Dashwood was now as certain of the colonel's excellent character as she had once been of Willoughby's, and hoped that Marianne would, in time, come to accept Colonel Brandon's offer of marriage.

Chapter Ten

Return to Barton

Marianne recovered so well that within a week she was able to travel home, with her mother and Elinor, in Colonel Brandon's carriage. Elinor was pleased to see that Marianne showed a new firmness of mind and calmness of expression. Although she was clearly still upset when she thought of the past, she was now able to control her feelings, and show a cheerful face to her family. She started planning a new life for herself.

'When I am stronger, Elinor, we will take long walks together every day. I shall never get up later than six, and I shall spend every morning practising my music or reading.'

Elinor smiled, doubting whether this plan would last very long, but happy to see Marianne enthusiastic again.

A couple of days later, the weather was so fine that Mrs Dashwood encouraged Elinor to take Marianne out for a gentle walk, and the sisters set out along the quiet country road.

'There, exactly there,' said Marianne, pointing to the hill behind the house, 'is where I fell, and first saw Willoughby. I am thankful to find that I can see the place with so little pain! Can we talk on that subject now, do you think, Elinor?'

She was affectionately encouraged to speak openly.

'I know how badly I have behaved! My illness has given me time to think. I should never have been so incautious in my behaviour with Willoughby, and so impolite to other people. I know now that my own uncontrolled feelings caused my suffering, and even my illness was all my own fault. I have been unkind and unfair to almost everybody I know! – but especially to you, dearest Elinor. Did I follow your example? No! Did I help or comfort you, when *you* were suffering? No! I only thought of my own sorrow and my own broken heart.'

Elinor, impatient to calm her, praised her honesty.

'I can never forget Willoughby,' continued Marianne, 'but my memories no longer make me miserable. If I only knew that he did not *always* intend to deceive me, that he had some good in him, I would have much greater peace of mind.'

Elinor took a deep breath, and passed on to her sister what Willoughby had told her. Marianne said nothing, but tears ran down her face. They were now on their way back to the cottage, and as they reached the door, she kissed Elinor gratefully, whispered, 'Tell mama,' and went slowly upstairs.

When Mrs Dashwood heard the story, she expressed some pity for Willoughby. But for her, nothing could remove the guilt of his behaviour towards Eliza, and then Marianne.

In the evening, when they were all together, Marianne spoke again of Willoughby. 'I wish to tell you both,' she told her mother and Elinor, in a trembling voice, 'that what Elinor told me this morning was a great relief to me. I could never have been happy with him, after knowing all this.'

'I know, I know!' cried her mother. 'My Marianne, happy with a scoundrel like that? No!'

'Marianne, you consider the matter,' said Elinor, 'exactly as a sensible person should. And I expect you realize that marriage to him would have involved you in many troubles and disappointments. You would always have been poor, and perhaps your influence on his heart would have lessened, as he realized his selfish demands could not be met.'

'Selfish? Do you think him selfish?' said Marianne. 'Yes, you are right, it is true. How foolish I was!'

'I am more to blame than you, my child,' said Mrs Dashwood. 'I should have discovered his intentions earlier.'

During the next few days, Marianne continued to get stronger, and life at Barton fell back into the old routines.

Elinor grew impatient for some news of Edward, but the news arrived in a rather unexpected way. Mrs Dashwood's manservant, Thomas, had been sent to Exeter one morning on business, and on his return finished his report with these words:

'I suppose you know, madam, that Mr Ferrars is married.'

Marianne looked quickly at Elinor's white face, and burst into uncontrolled sobbing. Mrs Dashwood did not know which daughter to take care of first. She and Margaret led Marianne to another room, and then Mrs Dashwood hurried back to Elinor, who, although clearly upset, had been able to start questioning Thomas. At once Mrs Dashwood took that trouble upon herself.

'Who told you that Mr Ferrars was married, Thomas?'

'I saw him myself, madam, with his lady, Miss Steele, as her name was then. Miss Steele called to me from a carriage, and asked after the young ladies' health. Then she smiled and said she had changed her name since she was last in Devon.'

'Was Mr Ferrars in the carriage with her?'

'Yes, madam. He was sitting next to her, but I didn't see his face. And Mr Ferrars isn't a gentleman for talking much.'

'Did Mrs Ferrars look well?'

'Yes, madam, very well, and extremely happy.'

Thomas was then sent away, and Elinor and her mother sat in thoughtful silence. Mrs Dashwood now realized that Elinor had hidden her feelings for Edward, in order to spare her mother any unhappiness. She felt guilty that Marianne's suffering had taken up so much of her time, when her eldest daughter was probably just as much in need of her care and attention. Elinor herself was extremely miserable. She had always had a secret hope that something might happen to prevent his marrying Lucy. But now he really was married, and she could not bear the thought of it.

A few days later, a gentleman was seen riding up to their front door. At first Elinor thought it must be Colonel Brandon, but it was not him. In fact, it looked just like Edward. She looked again. It *was* Edward. She moved away from the window, and sat down. 'I *will* be calm. I *will* – *must* – be calm.'

Her mother and sisters had recognized Edward, too, but not a word was spoken, and they all waited in silence for their visitor to appear. He entered, looking pale, agitated, and afraid. Mrs Dashwood greeted him kindly, and wished him every happiness. He blushed, and said something no one could hear.

Elinor, desperately, began to talk about the weather. When she had finished expressing her extreme delight in the dryness of the season, a very awful pause took place. It was ended by Mrs Dashwood, who felt it necessary to hope that Mrs Ferrars was well. Edward replied hurriedly that she was.

Another pause.

'Is Mrs Ferrars in Plymouth?' asked Elinor, bravely.

'Plymouth!' he said, surprised. 'No, my mother is in London.'

'I meant,' said Elinor, taking up her sewing from the table, 'to ask about Mrs *Edward* Ferrars.'

He blushed, looked puzzled, hesitated, then said, 'Perhaps you mean – my brother – you mean Mrs *Robert* Ferrars.'

'Mrs *Robert* Ferrars!' repeated Marianne and Mrs Dashwood in the greatest astonishment. Elinor could not speak.

'Mrs Robert *Ferrars!*' repeated Marianne and Mrs Dashwood
in the greatest astonishment.

'Yes,' said Edward, hurriedly, 'you may not have heard that my brother is now married to – to – to Miss Lucy Steele.'

Elinor could sit there no longer. She ran out of the room, and as soon as the door was closed, burst into tears of happiness. Until then, Edward had avoided looking at her; now he watched her hurry away, and seemed to fall into a dream. At last, without saying a word, he got up, left the room, and walked out of the house.

Great was the astonishment he left behind him. One thing, however, was certain. Edward was now free, and it was not hard to guess how he would use this freedom. Walking about in the fresh air made him feel brave enough to return, and when they all sat down to tea at four o'clock, Edward had won his lady, gained her mother's permission, and was the happiest man alive.

His heart was now open to Elinor, with his weaknesses and mistakes confessed, and his boyish attachment to Lucy discussed with all the wise experience of a man of twenty-four.

'My engagement to Lucy certainly was foolish,' said he, 'but it would not have happened if my mother had allowed me to choose a profession. I had nothing to do, and no friends to advise me, so I imagined myself in love. When I met you, my dear Elinor, I realized at once how weak I had been.'

Elinor's mother and sisters were delighted; they could not love Edward enough, nor praise Elinor enough.

And Elinor – how can *her* feelings be described? From the moment of learning that Edward was free, to the moment of his asking her to marry him, her mind was in a storm. But when all doubt was past and she heard his voice expressing his deep love and affection for her, she knew her happiness was complete.

Edward stayed at the cottage for a week, and one of the first subjects of discussion was of course Lucy's marriage. It appeared that Robert had visited her several times, trying to persuade her to set Edward free. Lucy had realized that it was now Robert, not Edward, who would inherit his mother's fortune. Being of similarly selfish character, they were attracted to each other, and decided to get married with speed and secrecy.

Edward's mother was, naturally, horrified by Robert's marriage. She did not greatly approve of Edward's engagement to Elinor either, but in the end was persuaded to accept it, and even, rather unwillingly, gave Edward ten thousand pounds; she had given the same to Fanny on *her* marriage. This was much more than was expected by Edward and Elinor, who could now afford to marry very soon, and move into the vicar's house at Delaford.

There they were visited by all their friends and relations, who found them one of the happiest couples in the world. Even Mrs Ferrars came to visit them, although they were never favourites with her. That honour was reserved for Robert and Lucy, who, by endless attentions and respectful messages, finally regained their place in her heart. The whole of Lucy's behaviour in the matter may be seen as a most encouraging example of what self-interest can do to gain wealth and position. With Mrs Ferrars' generous help, Robert and Lucy lived in great comfort, often visiting John and Fanny Dashwood; only their frequent domestic disagreements spoiled their happiness.

Elinor's move to Delaford did not separate her from her family, as her mother and sisters spent half their time with her. Mrs Dashwood was anxious to bring Marianne and Colonel Brandon together, which was also Elinor's and Edward's wish.

Knowing how good, how kind the colonel was, and how fondly he was attached to her, what could Marianne do?

At the age of seventeen, she had believed that passionate feeling was the most important thing in life. She had had her heart broken, and learned to recover from it. Then at nineteen, with feelings of only warm friendship and respect, she agreed to marry a man she had once considered dull, and far too old for marriage!

But so it was. Colonel Brandon was now as happy as all those who loved him believed he deserved to be, and Marianne, who could never love by halves, came in time to love her husband as much as she had loved Willoughby.

Willoughby himself was saddened to hear of her marriage, but he did not die of a broken heart. He even managed to get some enjoyment out of life, as his wife was not always unpleasant, and his home not always uncomfortable. But Marianne remained his idea of the perfect woman, and he often refused to admire a new young beauty as 'nothing to compare with Mrs Brandon'.

Mrs Dashwood stayed on at Barton Cottage, and as Margaret soon grew old enough for dancing and falling in love, Sir John and Mrs Jennings did not miss Elinor and Marianne as much as they had feared. Barton and Delaford were connected by strong family affection, and there was constant communication between the two places. Elinor and Marianne lived in great happiness, loved and respected by their husbands, and almost within sight of each other. The passing of the years only served to bring them all closer together.

GLOSSARY

admire *(v)* to have a very good opinion of someone or something

affection *(n)* a strong feeling of liking or love; **affectionate** *(adj)*

agitated *(adj)* showing in your behaviour that you are anxious and nervous

approve *(v)* to think that someone or something is good or right

astonish *(v)* to surprise someone very much

attachment *(n)* a feeling of liking or love for a place or person

attract *(v)* to cause a person to like someone

attractiveness *(n)* the appearance or qualities that make a person pleasant to look at or to be with

bachelor *(n)* an unmarried man

bear *(v)* to suffer pain or unhappiness; to accept something unpleasant without complaint

blush *(v)* to become red in the face, especially when embarrassed

carriage *(n)* a vehicle, pulled by horses, for carrying people

the Church *(n)* the Anglican Church (the Church of England)

comfort *(n)* having a pleasant life, with everything you need

comfort *(v)* to be kind and sympathetic to someone who is worried or unhappy

cottage *(n)* a small, simple house, usually in the country

debt *(n)* money that is owed to someone

debtor *(n)* a person who owes money

deceive *(v)* to make someone believe something that is not true

deserve *(v)* to be good enough, or worthy enough, for something

duel *(n)* a formal fight with weapons between two people, used in the past to decide an argument, often about a question of honour

elegant *(adj)* graceful and attractive in appearance; **elegance** *(n)*

fair *(adj)* treating people equally or in the right way

firm *(adj)*   strong and determined in attitude and behaviour

frost *(n)*   a thin white covering of ice on the ground in cold weather

gain *(v)*   to obtain or win something that you need or want

gentleman *(n)*   a man of good family and social position

Good heavens!   an exclamation of surprise

honour *(n)*   (1) the quality of knowing and doing what is morally right; (2) a great pleasure or privilege

hospitable *(adj)*   welcoming and generous to guests and visitors

infection *(n)*   an illness which can easily be passed on to others

inheritance *(n)*   money or property that you receive from someone when they die; **inherit** *(v)*

lack *(v & n)*   not having something, or not having enough of something

living *(n)*   *(in the past)* a position in the Church as a priest, and the income and house that go with this

lock *(n)*   a length or curl of hair

mistress *(n)*   *(in the past)* the female head of a house, who employs the servants

mother-in-law *(n)*   the mother of your husband or wife

opportunity *(n)*   a chance, the right time for doing something

passion *(n)*   a strong feeling or emotion, especially of love or hate; **passionate** *(adj)*

praise *(v & n)*   to express your admiration and good opinion of someone

recover *(v)*   to get better after an illness; **recovery** *(n)*

relieved *(adj)*   glad that a problem has gone away; **relief** *(n)*

respect *(v & n)*   to admire and have a high opinion of someone because of their good qualities

rival *(n)*   someone who competes with another person (e.g. in love)

romantic *(adj)* very imaginative and emotional; not looking at situations in a realistic way

scoundrel *(n)* a man who treats other people badly, especially by being dishonest or immoral

seduce *(v)* to persuade someone (usually young and inexperienced) to do something that is not sensible

sensibility *(n)* the ability to understand and experience deep feelings; the quality of being strongly affected by emotional influences

sink *(v)* to move downwards (e.g. by sitting or falling)

sob *(v)* to cry loudly and very unhappily

sociable *(adj)* fond of being with other people; friendly

sorrow *(n)* a feeling of great sadness

spoil *(v)* to do too much for a child, so that it has a bad effect on their character; **spoilt** *(adj)*

stepmother *(n)* the woman who is married to your father, but who is not your real mother

subject *(n)* the thing or person that is being discussed

taste *(n)* the ability to choose or recognize things which are elegant, attractive, and pleasing

trust *(v)* to have confidence in someone, and in their ability to keep a secret

vicar *(n)* a priest in the Church of England

vulgar *(adj)* low, common, coarse, lacking in taste or manners

ACTIVITIES

Before Reading

1 **Read the back cover of the book, and the story introduction on the first page. Can you guess which of these ideas are true?**

1 Both Elinor and Marianne suffer because...
   a they fall in love with unsuitable men.
   b they are too poor to attract interesting men.
   c they are both deceived by their admirers.
   d they fall in love with the same man.

2 Eventually the two sisters...
   a move back into their family home.
   b inherit their half-brother's fortune.
   c confess their guilty secret.
   d become more like each other.
   e marry for love.

2 **Read the back cover of the book again, and say whether you agree or disagree with these statements, and why.**

1 People with practical common-sense opinions are usually quite boring.
2 People who are full of passionate and romantic feeling all the time are very amusing.
3 True love can only be felt by the young. Middle-aged people cannot expect to fall in love.
4 Everyone should marry by the age of thirty-five.
5 Love is the most important thing in a woman's life; work, or sport, is the most important thing in a man's.

ACTIVITIES

While Reading

Read Chapters 1 to 3. Who said this, and to whom? What, or who, were they talking about?

1 'I would not wish to do anything mean.'
2 'One feels one's fortune is not one's own.'
3 'How shall we manage without her?'
4 'It is too early in life to lose hope of happiness.'
5 'Surely you must accept that he still has the full use of his arms and legs?'
6 'How cold, how calm their last goodbyes were!'
7 'Yes, he is well worth catching.'
8 'In spite of your very sensible opinion, I shall go on disliking him for ever!'
9 'Your sister, I understand, does not approve of second attachments.'
10 'I have such a secret to tell you.'
11 'I have found you out, miss, in spite of your cleverness.'
12 'Promise me you will change nothing, nothing at all!'

Before you read Chapter 4 (*Departures and Arrivals*), can you guess the answers to these questions?

1 Who is going to depart?
2 Who is going to arrive?
3 Are Marianne and Willoughby going to tell everyone about their engagement?
4 Why was Colonel Brandon called away so suddenly?

Read Chapters 4 to 6. Are these sentences true (T) or false (F)?
Rewrite the false sentences with the correct information.

1 Willoughby was planning to return to Devonshire very soon.
2 Elinor could not explain Willoughby's strange behaviour
   although she was confident that his intentions were honourable.
3 Edward Ferrars would rather be a vicar than a lawyer.
4 The lock of hair in Edward's ring belonged to his sister Fanny.
5 The Steele sisters were very fond of Lady Middleton's
   children.
6 Lucy Steele and Edward Ferrars had been secretly engaged for
   four years.
7 Elinor realized that Lucy was warning her to keep away from
   Edward.
8 Elinor told her family about Edward's secret engagement at
   once.
9 Marianne was anxious to see Colonel Brandon in London.
10 At the party in London, Willoughby spoke warmly and
   passionately to Marianne.
11 Willoughby decided to marry for money, to pay his debts.
12 Mrs Jennings was understanding about Willoughby's
   behaviour.

Before you read Chapter 7 (*The Truth about Willoughby*), can you
guess what the truth about Willoughby might be? Mark each of
these possibilities Y (Yes) or N (No).

1 He already has a wife.
2 He has seduced a young girl.
3 He has much larger debts than anyone imagined.
4 He has killed someone in a duel.
5 He has stolen money from his cousin, Mrs Smith.

Read Chapters 7 to 9. Choose the best question-word for these questions, and then answer them.

Why / What / Who

1 … was Marianne so upset when her mother's first letter arrived?
2 … did Colonel Brandon tell Elinor about Willoughby's past?
3 … relation to Colonel Brandon was the girl who was seduced by Willoughby?
4 … fought a duel over this girl?
5 … did John Dashwood advise Elinor to do?
6 … did Mrs Ferrars choose as a wife for Edward?
7 … told Fanny Dashwood about Lucy's engagement to Edward?
8 … made Marianne realize that Elinor was capable of real feeling?
9 … did Mrs Ferrars decide to leave her fortune to Robert, instead of Edward?
10 … offered a living to Edward?
11 … was the reason for Marianne's illness at Cleveland?
12 … did Willoughby come to Cleveland?

Before you read Chapter 10 (*Return to Barton*), what do you think is going to happen? Choose some of these ideas.

1 Marianne decides that she will never marry, and Elinor marries Colonel Brandon.
2 Lucy finds a richer husband, so Edward is free to marry Elinor.
3 Mrs Dashwood marries Colonel Brandon.
4 Willoughby's wife dies, and Marianne marries Willoughby.
5 Both sisters make happy marriages.

ACTIVITIES

After Reading

1 **Here are some thoughts of characters in the story. Decide which characters they are, and describe what is happening at this point in the story. Then explain what the remarks show about each character, and their opinion of others.**

1 'How sad to see those fine dinner plates go! What possible use will *they* have for things of such high quality? And that piano! It looks very well in a large sitting-room like the one here, but is most unsuitable for a little country cottage…'

2 'Miss Grey will have me, I'm sure of it. Fifty thousand a year! No more worries about debts, no need to sell my horses… I'm sorry about Marianne, but it's not my fault. I can't bear to be poor, and if Mrs Smith won't allow me any more money…'

3 'Now I've met her, I can see I was right to be worried. She's just the type Edward would admire. The poor fool talks about her far too often. But she can't have him – because he's mine!'

4 'She's dancing with him again. Look at that smile! She never smiles at me like that. I suppose it's natural. He's young, good-looking, self-confident, sociable… What chance do I have?'

5 'What a scoundrel I am, for lying to her about that ring! I ought to tell her the truth, go away, and never see her again – but I can't bear it. Oh, why was I such a fool, four years ago!'

6 'I do believe I've encouraged him to do it! Yes, he's going over to speak to her now. I mustn't listen, of course, but… yes, she's blushing! Oh, how wonderful! I'm sure they'll make each other very happy. I'm delighted for them both.'

2 **Marianne tells Elinor that Willoughby has offered to give her a horse (see page 25). Here is the conversation between Marianne and Elinor. Complete Marianne's side of the conversation.**

ELINOR: Marianne, what's happened? You look very excited!
MARIANNE: _____

ELINOR: Last night? No, I can't possibly guess. Just tell me!
MARIANNE: _____

ELINOR: A horse? Willoughby promised you that? Marianne, what *are* you thinking of?
MARIANNE: _____

ELINOR: You mean you intend to go riding with Willoughby – just the two of you?
MARIANNE: _____

ELINOR: You *must* know what's wrong with that. People will talk. In any case, you cannot accept a horse as a present.
MARIANNE: _____

ELINOR: Because it would be such an expensive gift! People would think there was an understanding between you and Willoughby.
MARIANNE: _____

ELINOR: I know it's not their business, but people still talk.
MARIANNE: _____

ELINOR: Yes, I do understand how much you want it. But where will you keep it? How much will it cost to feed, to look after?
MARIANNE: _____

ELINOR: You know very well mama couldn't possibly afford it.
MARIANNE: _____

ELINOR: I think you'll find that is the right decision, Marianne.

3 In this story, Elinor's actions and reactions are usually considered to represent 'sense', while Marianne's represent 'sensibility'. Look at the two examples given below, and add as many as you can to the list.

SENSE
• After her father's death, Elinor hides her deep sadness in order to discuss business with her brother and be polite to his wife.

SENSIBILITY
• Marianne falls in love with Willoughby because of his attractive appearance and romantic behaviour.

Do you think either sister has changed by the end of the story? If so, how much? Do you think the changes will last?

4 Here is the letter that Marianne writes to Willoughby after she meets him in London. Choose one suitable word to fill each gap.

Willoughby, how could you _____ to me like that _____ night? You were obviously _____ to speak to me, _____ my hand, or spend _____ time with me at _____. You turned away as _____ as you could. What _____ I done? Are you _____ with me? You know _____ well how much you _____ to me. I've never _____ my feelings for you, _____ perhaps this was rather _____. But you showed your _____ for me in so _____ ways. I cannot understand _____ has changed you! I _____ not changed.

   I must _____ you to reply at _____. I am ill with _____! My heart is simply _____! Willoughby, have you no _____? If I really mean _____ to you any more, _____ return all of my _____, and the lock of _____ which you begged me _____ give you.

   Marianne

5 **Do you agree or disagree with these statements about the characters in the story? Discuss your answers.**

1 In those times, marriage was a practical business, so Lucy, being poor, was right to try to find the richest husband she could.

2 Willoughby was not completely to blame for Marianne's broken heart. She should have been more cautious about allowing herself to fall in love with him.

3 Edward should have been open about his feelings for Elinor, and broken his engagement to Lucy.

4 Elinor knew that Lucy saw her as a rival, not as a friend, so there was no need for Elinor to keep Lucy's secret.

6 **Here is the beginning of an alternative ending to the novel (see page 83). Complete the ending in your own words, giving your opinions about whether these marriages will be successful or not.**

Elinor grew impatient for some news of Edward, and it was not long before the Dashwoods heard that he and Lucy were married. Elinor had prepared herself for this moment, and was able to remain calm, despite Marianne's sympathetic sobbing. She found most relief in the company of Colonel Brandon, who came regularly to Barton to comfort her. In fact, as Mrs Jennings had hoped, the understanding between them grew into a real attachment. Very soon, the colonel, having realized Marianne could never love him, asked Elinor to do him the honour of marrying him, and was accepted.

Several months after Elinor's wedding, news came of Mrs Willoughby's sudden death in a riding accident. Marianne found herself thinking of Willoughby more and more, and when he arrived at Barton one day…

Which ending do you prefer – this one, or the one in the story? Explain why.

ABOUT JANE AUSTEN

Jane Austen was born in 1775 at Steventon in Hampshire, in the south of England. She was the sixth of seven children of a clergyman, the Reverend George Austen. He was a well-educated man, who encouraged Jane in both her reading and her writing. In 1801, the family moved to Bath; then, after George Austen's death, to Southampton, and finally to Chawton in Hampshire (the house where Jane lived can still be visited). She led a quiet, uneventful life, occasionally visiting London, Bath, Lyme, and her brothers' houses. She never married, though she had several admirers. One proposal of marriage she accepted, but the next day changed her mind and withdrew her acceptance. Little is known about her love affairs, as her sister Cassandra was careful to edit Jane's private letters after her death, but it seems likely that Jane experienced disappointment in love and that she refused to marry without it. However, her life was spent in a close and affectionate family circle, and she was a much-loved aunt to her many nieces and nephews. She died in Winchester in 1817, aged only forty-two.

She started writing when she was only fourteen, and by her early twenties was already working on the first versions of some of her novels. She did not write about great events, like the French Revolution or the Napoleonic Wars, both of which happened during her lifetime. She wrote about what she knew best – the daily business of social visits, romantic affairs, and matchmaking. In a letter to a niece, she wrote, 'Three or four families in a country village is the very thing to work on.' And in a reply to a suggestion for the subject of her next novel, she explained that she could not write anything without 'laughing at myself or at other people'. With characteristic modesty, she finished, 'No, I must keep to my own style and go on in my own way; and though I may never succeed again in that, I am convinced that I should totally fail in any other.'

Her six major novels are now classics of English literature. They are *Sense and Sensibility, Pride and Prejudice, Mansfield Park, Emma, Northanger Abbey*, and *Persuasion*. Of these, *Mansfield Park, Emma*, and *Persuasion* were written in the busy parlour at Chawton, in the middle of the usual family activities and interruptions. *Sense and Sensibility* (1811) was the first to be published, and was based on an earlier sketch entitled *Elinor and Marianne*. According to her brother, Henry Austen, Jane was so modest about her writing that 'she could scarcely believe what she termed her great good fortune when Sense and Sensibility produced a clear profit of about £150.' Her novels were praised for their wit and style by readers of the time, and the Prince Regent (later King George IV) enjoyed them so much that he kept a complete set of her novels in each of his houses.

The novels have remained popular since they were first published, and there is a Jane Austen Society (known as the Janeites), which guards her literary reputation and her memory jealously. There have been film and television dramatizations of all the novels, in particular some very successful recent films of *Pride and Prejudice, Emma*, and *Sense and Sensibility*.

Jane Austen is one of the greatest novelists in the English language. Her novels are comedies of manners, dealing with parties, dresses, quarrels, engagements, and marriages, but no writer has ever drawn 'such pictures of domestic life in country villages' with a sharper eye or with a more exquisite irony.

OXFORD BOOKWORMS LIBRARY

Classics • Crime & Mystery • Factfiles • Fantasy & Horror
Human Interest • Playscripts • Thriller & Adventure
True Stories • World Stories

The OXFORD BOOKWORMS LIBRARY provides enjoyable reading in English, with a wide range of classic and modern fiction, non-fiction, and plays. It includes original and adapted texts in seven carefully graded language stages, which take learners from beginner to advanced level. An overview is given on the next pages.

All Stage 1 titles are available as audio recordings, as well as over eighty other titles from Starter to Stage 6. All Starters and many titles at Stages 1 to 4 are specially recommended for younger learners. Every Bookworm is illustrated, and Starters and Factfiles have full-colour illustrations.

The OXFORD BOOKWORMS LIBRARY also offers extensive support. Each book contains an introduction to the story, notes about the author, a glossary, and activities. Additional resources include tests and worksheets, and answers for these and for the activities in the books. There is advice on running a class library, using audio recordings, and the many ways of using Oxford Bookworms in reading programmes. Resource materials are available on the website <www.oup.com/elt/gradedreaders>.

The *Oxford Bookworms Collection* is a series for advanced learners. It consists of volumes of short stories by well-known authors, both classic and modern. Texts are not abridged or adapted in any way, but carefully selected to be accessible to the advanced student.

You can find details and a full list of titles in the *Oxford Bookworms Library Catalogue* and *Oxford English Language Teaching Catalogues*, and on the website <www.oup.com/elt/gradedreaders>.

THE OXFORD BOOKWORMS LIBRARY
GRADING AND SAMPLE EXTRACTS

STARTER • 250 HEADWORDS

present simple – present continuous – imperative –
can/cannot, must – *going to* (future) – simple gerunds ...

Her phone is ringing – but where is it?

Sally gets out of bed and looks in her bag. No phone. She
looks under the bed. No phone. Then she looks behind the
door. There is her phone. Sally picks up her phone and
answers it. *Sally's Phone*

STAGE 1 • 400 HEADWORDS

... past simple – coordination with *and*, *but*, *or* –
subordination with *before*, *after*, *when*, *because*, *so* ...

I knew him in Persia. He was a famous builder and I
worked with him there. For a time I was his friend, but
not for long. When he came to Paris, I came after him –
I wanted to watch him. He was a very clever, very
dangerous man. *The Phantom of the Opera*

STAGE 2 • 700 HEADWORDS

... present perfect – *will* (future) – *(don't) have to, must not, could* –
comparison of adjectives – simple *if* clauses – past continuous –
tag questions – *ask/tell* + infinitive ...

While I was writing these words in my diary, I decided what
to do. I must try to escape. I shall try to get down the wall
outside. The window is high above the ground, but I have
to try. I shall take some of the gold with me – if I escape,
perhaps it will be helpful later. *Dracula*

... should, may – present perfect continuous – *used to* – past perfect –
causative – relative clauses – indirect statements ...

Of course, it was most important that no one should see
Colin, Mary, or Dickon entering the secret garden. So Colin
gave orders to the gardeners that they must all keep away
from that part of the garden in future. *The Secret Garden*

... past perfect continuous – passive (simple forms) –
would conditional clauses – indirect questions –
relatives with *where/when* – gerunds after prepositions/phrases ...

I was glad. Now Hyde could not show his face to the world
again. If he did, every honest man in London would be proud
to report him to the police. *Dr Jekyll and Mr Hyde*

... future continuous – future perfect –
passive (modals, continuous forms) –
would have conditional clauses – modals + perfect infinitive ...

If he had spoken Estella's name, I would have hit him. I was
so angry with him, and so depressed about my future, that I
could not eat the breakfast. Instead I went straight to the old
house. *Great Expectations*

... passive (infinitives, gerunds) – advanced modal meanings –
clauses of concession, condition

When I stepped up to the piano, I was confident. It was as if I
knew that the prodigy side of me really did exist. And when I
started to play, I was so caught up in how lovely I looked that
I didn't worry how I would sound. *The Joy Luck Club*